COLORFUL
COMPONENTS

PATRICIA PARKER

STITCH
DAZZLING
DESIGNS
WITH
MULTI-HOLE
BEADS

Kalmbach
Media

DEDICATION

To my mother JoAnn and grandmother Evelyn,
who shared with me their love of needlework.

Kalmbach Media
21027 Crossroads Circle
Waukesha, Wisconsin 53186
www.JewelryAndBeadingStore.com

Published in 2019
23 22 21 20 19   1 2 3 4 5

Manufactured in China

ISBN: 978-1-62700-692-7
EISBN: 978-1-62700-693-4

Editor: Erica Barse
Book Design: Lisa Schroeder
Technical Editor: Jane Danley Cruz
Photographer: William Zuback

Library of Congress Control Number: 2018967272

CONTENTS

INTRODUCTION

Working with multi-hole beads is like working with a model building set. Each design is unique, depending on which bead you choose to use. The trick is to use each hole like it is a separate bead. So much of traditional stitched seed bead work depends on your chosen pattern and colors, but many shapes of multi-hole beads can be worked in the same color for a visually exciting end result.

When designing projects with multi-hole beads, I keep this formula in mind:
- The first hole is for stringing.
- The second hole is for making connections.
- The third hole will stabilize connections.
- The fourth hole is used for embellishing.

You can use this formula to create your own designs with any multi-hole beads of your choice. Many of these beads are interchangeable, and everything you do differently will achieve a uniquely beautiful result. With more and more new beads coming out all the time, the design possibilities are endless!

— Patricia

BASICS

THREAD

No thread is 100% perfect. Nylon works well in most cases. Some people prefer Fireline or the equivalent. Use whatever is best for you.

Tension, on the other hand, makes a huge difference. Some projects need to be worked with extremely tight tension, such as the Lantern Earrings on p. 62. Making sure your beads are as tight as can be will ensure your product is solid. Some projects, such as the Lace Doily Earrings on p. 78, require loose tension so the beads can settle into their place.

Sewing through any round again will even out your thread tension for the most part. If it's too loose, it'll tighten up; if it's too tight, you'll want to ease off a bit. I suggest working with an even, medium tension. Consistency is the most important thing to remember with your tension. Conditioning your thread can also help; however, any thread conditioner will tend to gunk up your beads, making subsequent passes more difficult. Also hair, fibers, and dust tend to get caught in the wax. Use it at your discretion.

TYING KNOTS

The most useful knot in beading is the half-hitch knot. Sewing around a current line of thread, and tie a knot up against a bead with a larger hole so that you can pull the knot through the hole and still pass through the bead afterward. When working with multi-hole beads, I like to tie a knot after the second or third pass through a bead before changing directions. This ensures that if the thread is frayed by a rough bead hole, the row will still hold.

Reinforcing, or sewing back through the bead path one or twice before you tie your knot, secures and firms up your beadwork. Sewing through a few beads again after you tie your knot will also help make your beadwork even more secure.

End a thread by sewing back through your beadwork, tying a few half-hitch knots as you go, and trimming the thread once you feel the beadwork is secure.

BEADS

Working with beads requires you to involve your fingers. Each design is built up with various multi-hole beds. As you build, use your fingers to form the beads into the shape you want them to be. Hold onto the beads by pinching between your thumb and your forefinger to really control what they do rather than let them control you.

I prefer to work with Toho seed beads because they have the largest inside hole, which allows for more passes and easier passage as you sew. When working with multi-hole beads, be sure to check all of the holes for blockage before you start working with them. I do this by just sewing my needle through the bead I intend to use as I pick it up. Note that some of the finishes on these beads are not as permanent as one would like. Make sure you test the beads you're using before you make a huge project with them.

NOTE: Having finish wear off is really frustrating. Paint-on lacquer is available, if you want a more permanent finish. It's best to use this product after your beadwork is finished so you do not inadvertently block the bead holes. And use the colors you like—when working (and especially when designing!), using colors you like will make learning easier.

RESOURCES

My local retailer is Owl Be Beading in Bethlehem, Pennsylvania. Potomac beads (potomacbeads. com) and Twisted Sistah (twistedsistahbeads. com) carry the shaped beads needed to make the projects in this book, and Bobby Bead (bobbybead.com) is an excellent source for Toho seed beads. Ask your local bead store for The BeadSmith (beadsmith.com) products.

BEAD KEY

- 11º seed beads
- 11º cylinder beads
- 8º seed beads
- 6mm two-hole cabochons
- 6mm DiscDuo beads
- 6mm honeycomb beads
- 5x8mm PaisleyDuo beads
- 2x5mm, 3x6mm, and 4x8mm Infinity beads
- 5mm GemDuo beads
- 6x2mm bar beads
- 5x2mm StormDuo beads
- 9x5mm Kite beads
- 4mm Es-o beads
- 8mm octo beads
- 3x6mm and 4x8mm Trinity beads
- 6x3mm eMMA beads
- 10x3mm beam beads

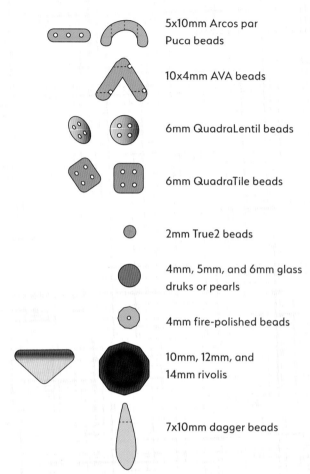

- 5x10mm Arcos par Puca beads
- 10x4mm AVA beads
- 6mm QuadraLentil beads
- 6mm QuadraTile beads
- 2mm True2 beads
- 4mm, 5mm, and 6mm glass druks or pearls
- 4mm fire-polished beads
- 10mm, 12mm, and 14mm rivolis
- 7x10mm dagger beads

ORIENTATION

The holes in the four-hole beads will be labeled differently for each project, depending on the order in which they are used.

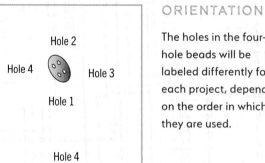

Hole 2
Hole 4   Hole 3
Hole 1

Hole 4
Hole 3   Hole 2
Hole 1

 8
 10
 13
 16

 19
 22
 26
 29

 33
 37
 40
 43

 46
 49
 52

PROJECTS

 55
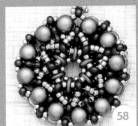 58
 62
 65

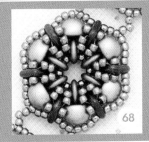 68
 71
 75
 78

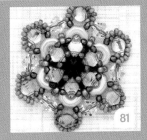 81
 85
 89
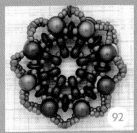 92

This basic chain is perfect for displaying a beautiful beaded pendant (see the "Five-Star Bracelet," p. 71).

COBBLESTONES CHAIN

MAKE THE CHAIN

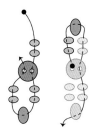

1. Thread a needle on a comfortable length of thread, pick up two 11º seed beads, a mini Round-Duo bead, two 11ºs, an 8º seed bead, and two 11ºs, and sew through the open hole of the mini RoundDuo, leaving an 8-in. (20cm) tail. Pick up two 11ºs and an 8º, and sew through the first two 11ºs added, the mini RounDuo, and the next two 11ºs, and the 8º. This equals one unit. Exit the 8º.

2. Continue to add units until you reach the desired length, ending and adding thread as needed.

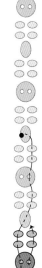

Supplies

Necklace, 20 in. (51cm)

- **10g** 11º seed beads in **2 colors**

- **3g** 8º seed beads

- **50** 4mm mini RounDuo beads

- **2** 4mm jump rings

- Clasp

- Beading needle and thread

- **2** pairs of chainnose pliers

FINISH THE PIECE

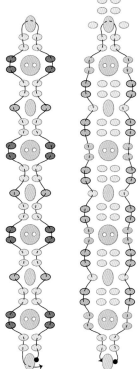

3. Work down the side of the chain using two 11ºs interspersed with mini RounDuos and one 11º interspersed with 8ºs (see note). With the thread exiting the 8º, continue through the next two 11ºs, and pick up two 11ºs (in the second color), skip the mini RounDuo, and sew through the next two 11ºs. Pick up an 11º, skip the 8º, and sew through the next two 11ºs in the chain. Repeat this stitch for both sides of the chain.

NOTE: For a necklace chain, only add the extra embellishment to the last six units; otherwise, the chain will not curve properly.

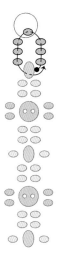

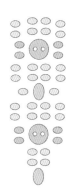

4. Exit an end 11º. Pick up seven 11ºs, and sew back through the last 11º to make a loop. Work back down the second side as in step 3. Add 11ºs between the outer row on both sides of bracelet. Add another loop of 11ºs at the other end of the chain, and end the threads. Attach a jump ring and clasp half to each beaded loop.

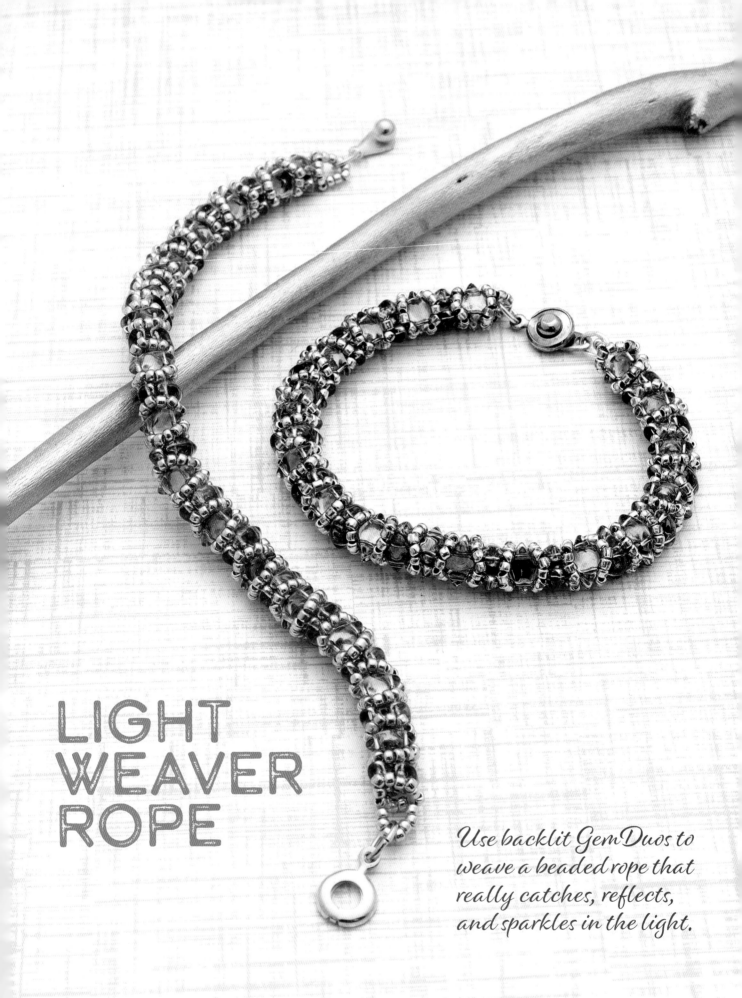

LIGHT
WEAVER
ROPE

Use backlit GemDuos to weave a beaded rope that really catches, reflects, and sparkles in the light.

MAKE THE ROPE

Supplies

Bracelet, 8 in. (20cm)

15g 11º seed beads

80 GemDuo beads

2 4mm jump rings

Clasp

Beading needle and thread

2 pairs of chainnose pliers

1. Thread a needle on a comfortable length of thread. Pick up 12 11º seed beads, and sew through the first 11º again to make a circle, leaving a 6-in. (15cm) tail. Sew through all the beads a second time to reinforce the thread path.

NOTE: For the following steps, always pick up each GemDuo bead so the reverse side is facing toward the inside of the beaded circle.

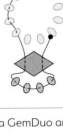

2. Pick up a GemDuo and four 11º s, and sew through the open hole of the same GemDuo and into the base circle, skipping two 11º s. Sew through the next seven 11º s.

3. Pick up a GemDuo and four 11º s, and sew through the open hole of the same GemDuo and into the base row, skipping two 11º s. Sew through the next six 11º s in the base row, and then continue through the next GemDuo and the four 11º s above the GemDuo.

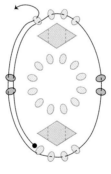

4. Pick up two 11º s, and sew through the four 11º s above the other GemDuo. Pick up two 11º s, and sew through the four 11º s above the first GemDuo, the first two 11º s added in this step, and the first bead in the next set of four 11º s.

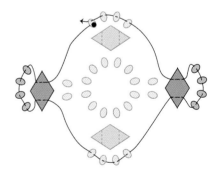

5. Pick up a GemDuo and four 11º s, and sew through the open hole of the same GemDuo. Sew through the four 11º s above the GemDuo added previously. Pick up a Gem-Duo and four 11º s, and sew through the second hole of the GemDuo and the four 11º s above the other GemDuo.

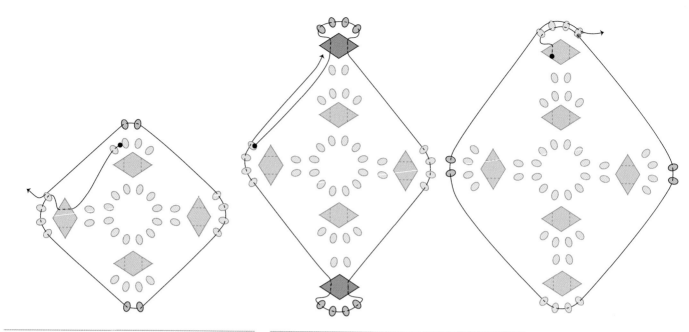

6. Step up through the adjacent GemDuo and the four 11ºs above that GemDuo. Pick up two 11ºs, and sew through the four 11ºs above the other GemDuo on the opposite side of the ring. Pick up two 11ºs, and sew through the first 11º over the first GemDuo sewn through in this step.

7. Repeat steps 5–6 until you reach the desired length. To add the clasp, exit the final 11º on one end of the rope, pick up five 11ºs, and sew back through the 11º you just exited to make a loop. Repeat on the other end of the rope, and end the threads. Attach a jump ring and half of the clasp to each beaded loop.

NOTE: This project can easily be worked using DiamonDuos for a slightly slimmer look. Or use 1-in. (2.5cm) links of the rope as beaded beads, and string with 8mm beads.

ART DECO BRACELET

A boldly highlighted edging adorns this component, which is reminiscent of geometric deco designs. Turn it into a bracelet or a great pair of earrings.

MAKE THE BRACELET

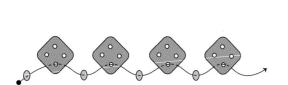

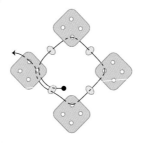

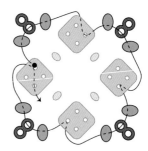

1. Thread a needle on a 50-in. (1.27m) length of thread, and pick up an 11º seed bead and a QuadraTile bead four times.

2. Sew through all the beads a second time to form a ring. Sew through the beads a third time, and tie a half-hitch knot with the tail. Sew through all the beads one final time, exit the last QuadraTile, and then sew through the adjacent (second) hole of the same QuadraTile.

3. Pick up an 8º seed bead, an Infinity bead, and an 8º and sew through the corresponding (second) hole of the next QuadraTile. Repeat this stitch three times. Sew through the beads just added a second time, keeping your tension even. Reinforce, and tie a half-hitch knot. Exit the last QuadraTile, and sew through the third hole of the same QuadraTile.

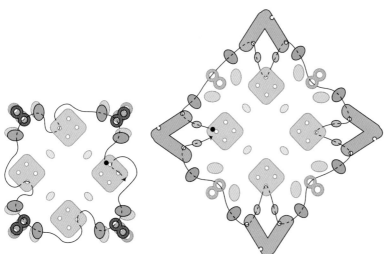

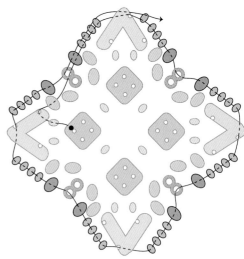

4. Turn the work over. Pick up an 8º, an Infinity, and an 8º, and sew through the corresponding (third) hole of the next QuadraTile. Repeat to complete the round.

5. Pick up an 11º, an AVA bead (inside to outside of hole 1), and an 8º, and sew through the open hole of the Infinity. Pick up an 8º, and sew through hole 2 (outside to inside) of the second AVA. Pick up an 11º, and sew through the open (fourth) hole of the next QuadraTile. Repeat these stitches three times. Exit the last QuadraTile.

6. Sew through the beadwork to exit the outer hole of the nearest Infinity. Pick up an 8º and four 11ºs, and then sew through the third hole of the AVA. Pick up an 8º and four 11ºs, and sew through the top hole of the next Infinity. Repeat these stitches three times, and exit the 11º after the third hole of the first AVA.

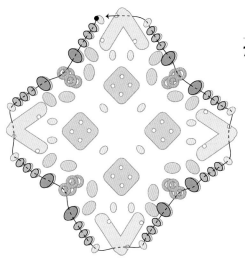

7. Turn the work over. Pick up three 11⁰s and an 8⁰, and sew through the open hole of the next Infinity. Pick up an 8⁰ and three 11⁰s, and sew through the 11⁰ before the AVA, the AVA (third hole), and the 11⁰ after the AVA. Repeat these stitches three times. Exit the last AVA. End the tail but not the working thread.

Repeat steps 1–7 to make five components.

FINISH THE BRACELET

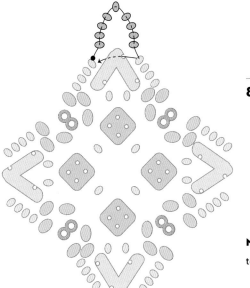

8. Thread a needle on the working thread of a component. Exit the 11⁰ after an AVA. Pick up nine 11⁰s, and sew through an 11⁰, AVA, and 11⁰ three-bead set to make a loop. Reinforce the beads twice, and end the threads. Repeat for another component.

NOTE: Simply add an ear wire at this point to make an earring, if desired.

Supplies

Bracelet, 8 in. (20cm)

5g 11⁰ seed beads

6g 8⁰ seed beads

20 3x6mm Infinity beads

20 QuadraTile beads

20 AVA beads

2 4mm oval jump rings

Clasp

Beading needle and thread

2 pair of chainnose pliers

ORIENTATION

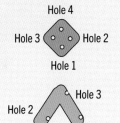

Hole 4
Hole 3   Hole 2
Hole 1

Hole 3
Hole 2
Hole 1

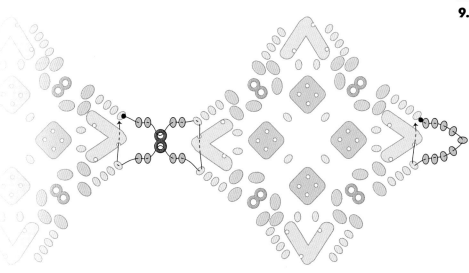

9. Attach the components together: With the first component (on the end opposite the loop), exit an 11⁰ after the AVA (third hole). Pick up two 11⁰s, an Infinity, and two 11⁰s, and sew through an 11⁰, AVA, and 11⁰ on a second component. Pick up two 11⁰s, sew through the open hole of the Infinity, pick up two more 11⁰s, and sew through the 11⁰, AVA, and 11⁰ on the first component. Repeat the thread path two times to reinforce. End the threads. Repeat this step to attach the remaining components. Attach a jump ring and clasp half to the loop on each end of the bracelet.

DESERT ROSE BRACELET

The dusky hues in this substantial bracelet remind me of sunsets in the American Southwest. I was also inspired by the mix of interesting bead shapes, which somehow all came together in beady harmony.

MAKE THE COMPONENTS

1. Thread a needle on a comfortable length of thread, and pick up a repeating pattern of an 11º seed bead and a QuadraLentil bead four times.

2. Sew through all of the beads again to make a circle, leaving a 4-in. (10cm) tail. Reinforce and secure this thread path by sewing through all of the beads again. Tie a half-hitch knot, and then sew through all of the beads once more. Exit a QuadraLentil, and sew through the opposite (second) hole of the same QuadraLentil.

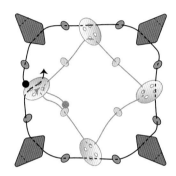

3. Pick up an 11º, a kite bead (wide end), and an 11º, and sew through the second hole of the next QuadraLentil. Repeat this stitch three times. Sew through all of the beads in this round again. Tie a half-hitch knot, sew through a few more beads, and exit a QuadraLentil. Sew through the adjacent (third) hole of the same QuadraLentil.

NOTE: It's helpful to make a visual check of your work to be sure you have not missed any holes and have the correct placement at this point.

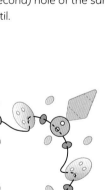

4. Pick up an 11º, an Es-o bead, and an 11º, and sew through the corresponding third hole of the next QuadraLentil. Repeat this stitch three times. Exit an Es-o.

Supplies

Bracelet, 7 in. (18cm)

5g 11º seed beads

 24 QuadraLentil beads

 48 StormDuo beads

 24 Kite beads

24 Es-o beads

 30 7mm two-hole cabochons

24 4mm pearls

2 4mm jump rings

Clasp

Beading needle and thread

2 pairs of chainnose pliers

ORIENTATION

Hole 2
Hole 4   Hole 3
Hole 1

Wide end

Tip end

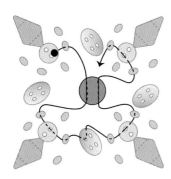

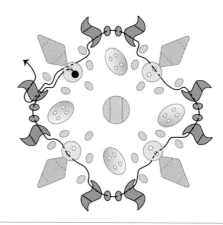

5. Working clockwise, sew through the next 11º, and pick up a two-hole cabochon (upper left hole, domed side up). Sew through the previous 11º, Es-o, and 11º, the second hole of the QuadraLentil, and the 11º, Es-o, and 11º. Sew through the lower right hole of the two-hole cab. Sew through the adjacent 11º, Es-o, and 11º, and then back through the same hole of the two-hole cab. Reinforce the thread path, and exit the Es-o your thread exited at the start of this step.

6. Sew through the open hole of the Es-o to begin working counter-clockwise. Pick up a StormDuo bead, two 11ºs, and a StormDuo, and sew through the open hole of the next Es-o. Repeat this stitch three times. Reinforce the thread path, and exit the StormDuo. Turn and sew through the open hole of the same StormDuo.

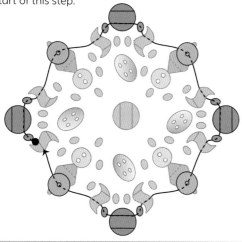

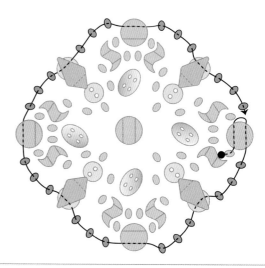

7. Pick up an 11º, a two-hole cab, and an 11º and sew through the open hole of the next StormDuo. Pick up a 4mm pearl, and sew through the open hole of the next StormDuo. Repeat these stitches three times. Reinforce, check your work, and then tie a half-hitch knot. Sew through a few more beads to exit a StormDuo.

8. Turn the beadwork over so you are working the back side. Sew through the next 11º and two-hole cab bead, then sew through the open hole of the same two-hole cab. Pick up three 11ºs, and sew through the open hole of the next kite. Pick up three 11ºs, and sew through the open hole of the next two-hole cab. Repeat these stitches three times. Reinforce, and then tie a half-hitch knot. Sew through a few beads to exit an 11º before a two-hole cab. Don't end the threads. Make a total of six components.

FINISH THE BRACELET

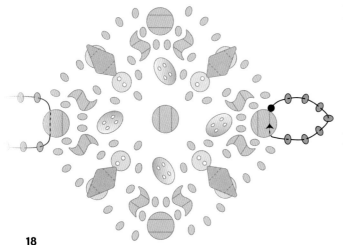

9. Exit a two-hole cab on one component, pick up three 11ºs, and sew through the outer hole of the two-hole cab on the second component. Pick up three 11ºs, and sew through the two-hole cab on the first component. Reinforce the thread path well, and tie a half-hitch knot. End the thread. Repeat this step to connect all the components.

10. On an end component, exit an outer hole of a two-hole cab, pick up seven 11ºs, and sew through the same hole of the two-hole cab. Reinforce, and end the thread. Repeat on the other end of the bracelet. Attach a jump ring and clasp half to each end loop.

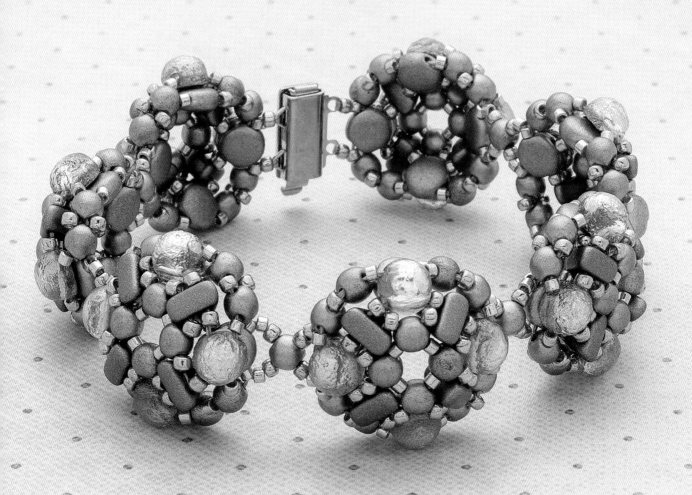

FAIRY RING BRACELET

A fairy ring is formed when mushrooms spread their spores in a circular pattern, resulting in a ring of new-growth mushrooms. The sparkly cute components that make up this bracelet could easily be mistaken for fantasy mushrooms.

MAKE THE COMPONENT

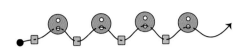

1. Thread a needle on a 50-in. (1.27m) piece of thread, and pick up a repeating pattern of an 11º cylinder bead and a mini RounDuo bead four times.

2. Sew through all of the beads again to make a circle, leaving a 6-in. (15cm) tail. Tie a half-hitch knot, sew through all of the beads again, and exit a mini RounDuo. Sew through the other hole of the same mini RounDuo.

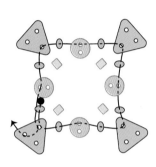

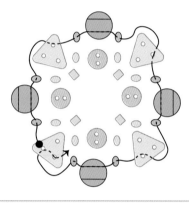

3. Pick up an 11º seed bead, an eMMA bead, and a seed bead, and sew through the open hole of the next mini RounDuo. Repeat this stitch three times. Reinforce the round. Exit the eMMA, and sew through the adjacent (second) hole of the same eMMA.

4. Working clockwise, pick up a seed bead, a two-hole cabochon, and a seed bead, and sew through the corresponding second hole of the next eMMA. Repeat this stitch three times, reinforce, and sew through the open hole of the same eMMA.

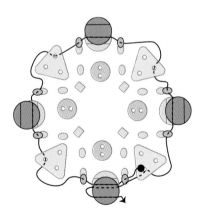

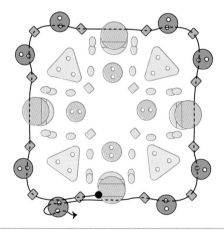

5. Flip the beadwork over. Pick up a seed bead, a DiscDuo, and a seed bead, and sew through the open hole of the next eMMA. Repeat this stitch three times, reinforce, and tie a half-hitch knot. Exit a mini DiscDuo, and sew through the open hole of the same mini DiscDuo.

6. Pick up a cylinder, a mini RounDuo, a cylinder, a mini RounDuo, and a cylinder, and sew through the open hole of the next DiscDuo. Repeat this stitch three times. This will cause the beadwork to dome, with the two-hole cabs on the upper side. Exit the mini RounDuo, turn, and sew through the other hole of the same bead.

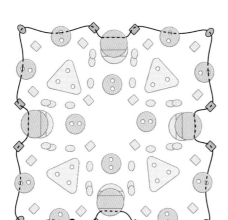

Supplies

Bracelet, 8 in. (20cm)

 5g 11º cylinder beads

5g 11º seed beads

 84 4mm mini RounDuo beads

 28 eMMA beads

28 two-hole cabochon beads

28 DiscDuo beads

2-loop clasp

Beading needle and thread

ORIENTATION

Hole 1

Hole 2   Hole 3

7. Pick up a cylinder, and sew through the outer hole of the DiscDuo. Pick up a cylinder, and sew through the open hole of the mini RounDuo. Pick up a seed bead, and sew through the open hole of the next mini RounDuo. Repeat these stitches three times. Reinforce, tie a half-hitch knot, and end the threads.

Make five more components.

FINISH THE BRACELET

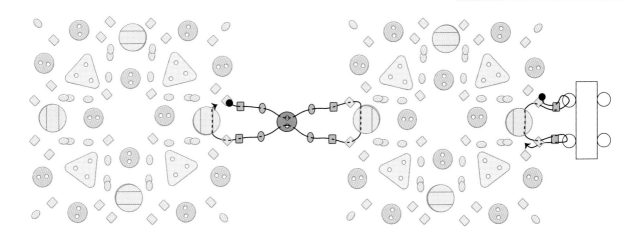

8. On one component, add a 10-in. (25cm) piece of thread and exit a cylinder after the two-hole cab. Pick up a cylinder, a seed bead, a mini RounDuo, a seed bead, and a cylinder, and sew through the corresponding cylinder and the outer hole of the two-hole cab on another component and a cylinder. Pick up a cylinder and a seed bead, and sew through the open hole of the mini RounDuo bead. Pick up a seed bead and a cylinder, and sew through a cylinder, a two-hole cab, and a cylinder on the first component. Reinforce. Attach a clasp half using a cylinder to connect each clasp loop: With the thread exiting a cylinder after a miniRounDuo, pick up a cylinder, and sew through the first loop of the clasp. Sew back through the two cylinders, the mini RounDuo, and the next (adjacent) cylinder. Pick up a cylinder, and sew through the second loop of the clasp, then continue back through the two cylinders and the miniRounDuo. Reinforce. Attach the second loop of the clasp to the other end of the bracelet. End the threads.

HOPSCOTCH NECKLACE

This tidy component is a solid square design that can be made reversible by using two different kinds of DiscDuos or honeycomb beads. You can also combine the two kinds of beads.

MAKE THE COMPONENT

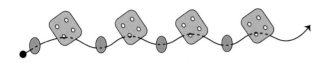

Supplies

Necklace, 20 in. (51cm)

3–5g 11⁰ seed beads

15–20g 8⁰ seed beads

48 QuadraTile beads

24 honeycomb or DiscDuo beads

24 two-hole cabochons

2 4mm jump rings and clasp

Beading needle and thread

2 pairs of chainnose pliers

ORIENTATION

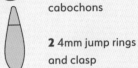

Hole 4

Hole 3   Hole 2

Hole 1

1. Thread a needle on a 50-in. (1.27m) piece of thread, and pick up a repeating pattern of an 8⁰ seed bead and a QuadraTile bead four times.

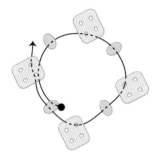

2. Sew through all of the beads again, leaving a 4-in. (10cm) tail. Tie a half-hitch knot, and sew through all the beads one more time. Exit a QuadraTile, and sew through the adjacent (second) hole of the QuadraTile.

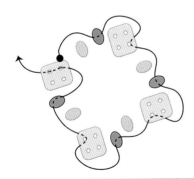

3. Pick up an 8⁰, and sew through the corresponding second hole of the next QuadraTile. Repeat this stitch three times. Reinforce. Exit the QuadraTile, and sew through the adjacent (fourth) hole of the same QuadraTile.

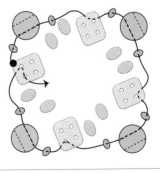

4. Pick up an 11⁰, a DiscDuo (or honeycomb) bead, and an 11⁰, and sew through the corresponding fourth hole of the next QuadraTile. Repeat this stitch three times. Sew through all of the beads again, exit the QuadraTile, and sew through the third hole of the same QuadraTile.

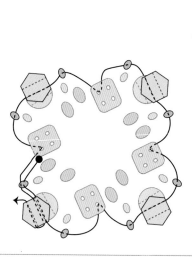

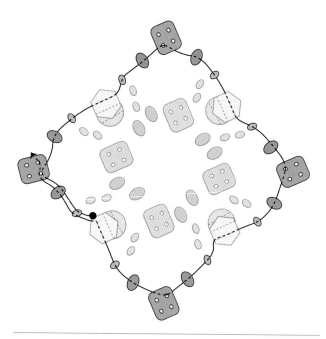

5. Pick up an 11º, a honeycomb (or DiscDuo) bead, and an 11º, and sew through the corresponding fourth hole of the next QuadraTile. Repeat this stitch three times. Reinforce. Exit the honeycomb, turn, and sew through the other hole of the same bead.

6. Pick up an 11º, an 8º, a QuadraTile, an 11º, and an 8º, and sew through the open hole of the next honeycomb. Repeat this stitch three times. Reinforce, exit the QuadraTile, and sew through the second hole of the same QuadraTile.

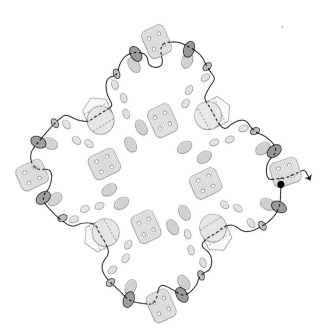

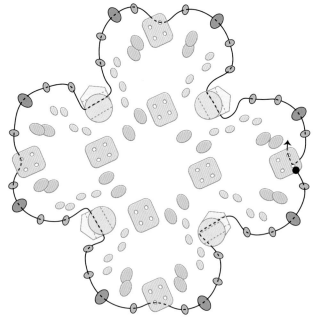

7. Flip the beadwork over. Pick up an 8º and an 11º, and sew through the open hole of the next DiscDuo. Pick up an 11º and an 8º, and sew through the corresponding second hole of the next QuadraTile. Repeat this stitch three times. Exit the third hole of the same QuadraTile.

8. Pick up an 11º, an 8º, and two 11ºs, and sew through the top hole of the next DiscDuo. Pick up two 11ºs, an 8º, and an 11º, and sew through the third hole of the next QuadraTile. Repeat these stitches three times. Exit the QuadraTile, turn, and sew through the open (fourth) hole of the same QuadraTile.

9. Flip the beadwork over. Pick up an 11º, and sew through the existing 8º. Pick up two 11ºs, and sew through the second hole of the next honeycomb. Pick up two 11ºs, and sew through the next 8º. Pick up an 11º, and sew through the open hole of the next QuadraTile. Repeat these stitches three times. Reinforce the row, and exit the 11º after a QuadraTile.

Make five more components.

FINISH THE NECKLACE

1. Start a herringbone chain from a corner of a component: Use the working thread on one component (or add a new thread). Pick up two 8ºs, sew through the corner 11º, QuadraLentil, and 11º, and continue up through the first 8º. Pick up two 8ºs, and sew through the second 8º added, the 11º, QuadraLentil, and 11º, the first 8º added, and the third 8º added. Pick up two 8ºs, sew through the second and fourth 8ºs, and continue through the first, third, and fifth 8ºs added. Continue to add 8ºs in this manner, two at a time, for a total of nine pairs of 8ºs. Then pick up an 11º, a honeycomb, and two 11ºs, and sew down through the second hole of the honeycomb. Pick up an 11º, and sew through the last set of 8ºs added, then continue through the first side of the beads just added. Continue to work in herringbone stitch using 8ºs (nine pairs), then add another grouping of an 11º, honeycomb, and 11º. Add as many pairs of 8ºs as needed to reach your desired length. Repeat with another component to make another neck strap.

2. See the project photo to connect the components into a necklace. Work as in step 1, but create five herringbone rows off of two 11ºs instead of an 11º, QuadraLentil, and 11º grouping. Sew through the adjacent two 11ºs on another component. Connect five components, including the two with attached neck straps, as shown.

3. Work as in step 1 to add two pairs of 8ºs to the final component and attach it to the bottom corner of the center component.

4. To add a clasp, exit the last set of 8ºs on the chain. Pick up seven 11ºs, and sew through the 8º next to the 8º your thread is exiting. Reinforce. Add jump rings and a clasp to the loop. Repeat on the other end of the necklace to finish the piece.

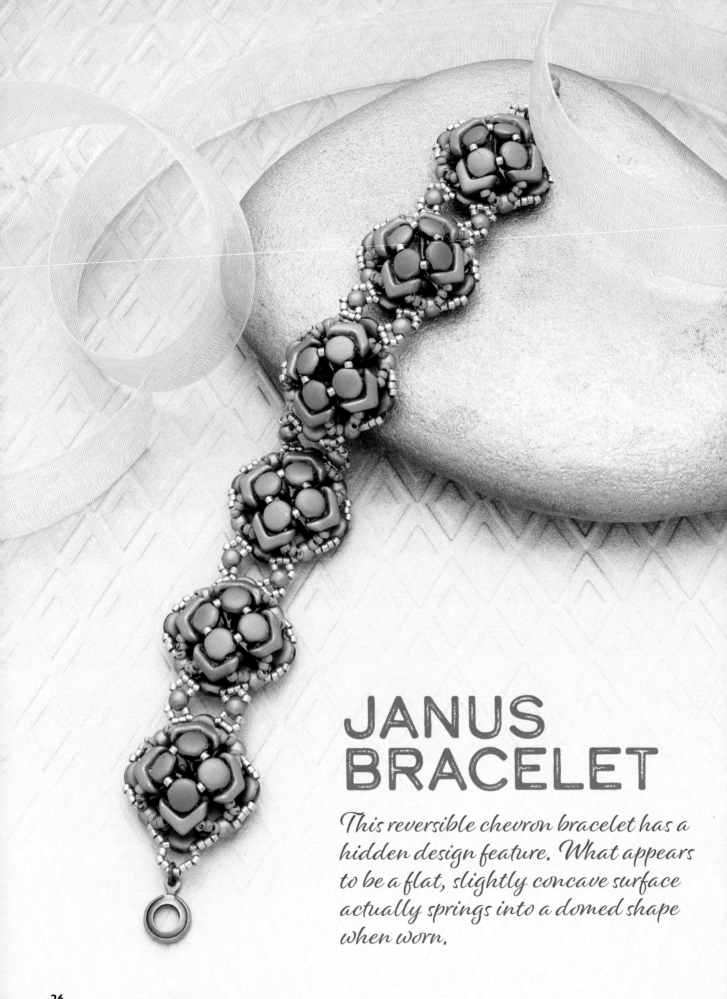

JANUS BRACELET

This reversible chevron bracelet has a hidden design feature. What appears to be a flat, slightly concave surface actually springs into a domed shape when worn.

MAKE THE COMPONENTS

Supplies

Bracelet, 8 in. (20cm)

5g 11° seed beads

5g 11° cylinder beads

20 AVA beads

40 DiscDuo beads

20 EVA beads

28 mini RounDuo beads

2 4mm jump rings

Clasp

Beading needle and thread

2 pairs of chainnose pliers

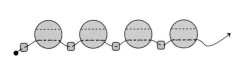

1. Thread a needle on a 50-in. (1.27m) piece of thread, and pick up an 11° cylinder bead and a DiscDuo bead four times.

2. Sew through all the beads again to make a circle, leaving a 6-in. (15cm) tail. Tie a half-hitch knot, and sew through all of the beads again. Exit the DiscDuo, turn, and sew through the other hole of the same DiscDuo.

ORIENTATION

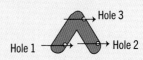

Hole 1   Hole 2

The smaller sized EVA bead has two holes that are vertical.

Hole 1 → → Hole 2 → Hole 3

The larger sized AVA bead has three holes that are horizontal.

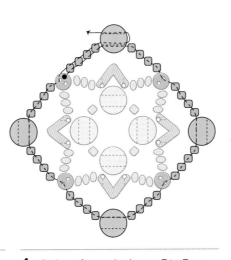

3. Pick up an EVA bead (inside hole), three 11°s, a mini RounDuo, three 11°s, and an EVA (outside hole), and sew through the open hole of the next DiscDuo. Repeat three times. Reinforce. Tie a half-hitch knot, sew through the beads to exit the mini RounDuo, turn, and continue through the other hole of the same mini RounDuo.

4. Pick up four cylinders, a DiscDuo, and four cylinders, and sew through the open hole of the next mini RounDuo. Repeat this stitch three times. Reinforce. Exit the DiscDuo, and sew through the other hole of the same DiscDuo.

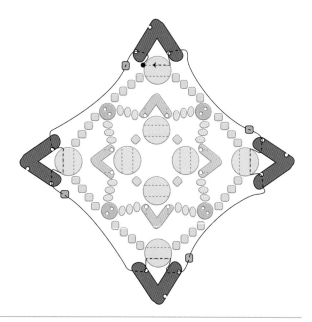

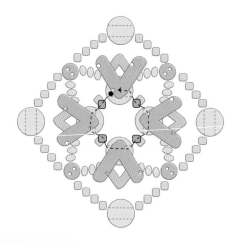

5. Pick up a color B AVA (inside hole), a cylinder, and a B (outside hole), and sew through the open hole of the next DiscDuo. Repeat this stitch three times. Reinforce. Exit a B, and sew through the tip hole of the same AVA.

6. With the thread exiting a tip hole of a B, pick up a cylinder and sew through the tip hole of the next B. Repeat this stitch three times. Repeat the thread path two times to reinforce well, and end the thread.

Make five more components.

FINISH THE BRACELET

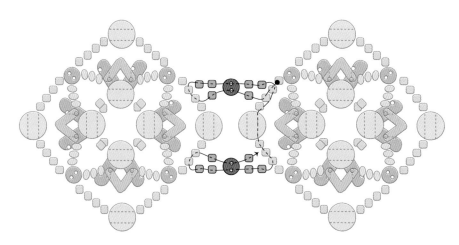

7. Thread a needle on a new 20 in. (51cm) piece of thread. Exit the third cylinder after a mini RounDuo in one component. Pick up a cylinder, a mini RounDuo, and a cylinder, and sew through the third and second cylinder after the DiscDuo on another component. Pick up two cylinders, and sew through the open hole of the mini RounDuo. Pick up two cylinders, and sew through the second and third beads from the first component. Reinforce twice. Continue through to the third cylinder on the other side of the same DiscDuo. Repeat this step, picking up two cylinders first, and then one cylinder for the final connection. Sew around the exterior of the component, exiting on the other side, and add another component. Repeat to add all the components, and end the threads.

8. On an end tile, exit the cylinder before the end DiscDuo. Pick up seven 11°s, and sew through the cylinder after the DiscDuo, the DiscDuo, and the cylinder before the DiscDuo. Reinforce, and end the thread. Repeat on the other end of the bracelet. Attach a jump ring and clasp half to each end loop.

MARRAKESH EARRINGS & BRACELET

A large, flat base supports interesting curved Arcos par Puca beads. These lightweight earrings and bracelet pack a serious visual punch.

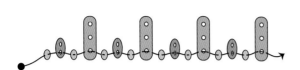

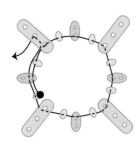

1. Thread a needle on a 50-in. (1.27m) length of thread, and pick up a repeating pattern of an 11º seed bead, an Es-o, an 11º, and a beam bead (end hole) four times.

2. Sew through all of the beads a second time to make a circle, leaving a 4-in. (10cm) tail. Tie a half-hitch knot, and sew through all of the beads again. Exit a beam, turn, and sew through the adjacent (second) hole of the same beam.

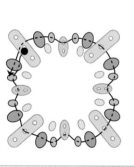

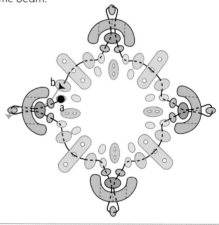

3. Pick up an 8º seed bead and an 11º, and sew through the open hole of the next Es-o. Pick up an 11º and an 8º, and sew through the second hole of the next beam. Repeat this stitch three times. Reinforce, and exit an 11º after an 8º.

4. a. Pick up an 11º, an 8º, an Arcos par Puca bead (center hole, concave side), and an 11º. Sew back through the Arcos (center hole) and the 8º, pick up an 11º, and sew through the next 11º, 8º, beam, 8º, and 11º on the base component. Repeat this stitch three times, working your way around the component back to the starting point of the round.
b. Sew through the first few beads added to exit an 11º at the apex of the Arcos.

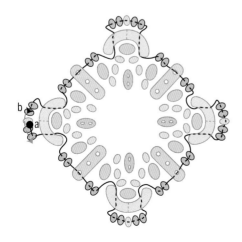

5. a. Pick up two 11ºs, and sew through the outer hole of the Arcos (convex side). Pick up two 11ºs, and sew through the open hole of the beam. Pick up two 11ºs, and sew through the outer hole of the next Arcos (concave side). Pick up two 11ºs, and sew through the 11º at the apex of the Arcos. Repeat these stitches three times.
b. Sew through two more 11ºs, and exit the first two 11ºs you added in this step.

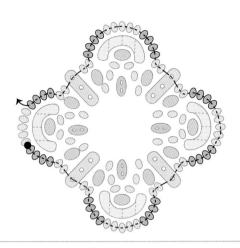

6. Pick up four 11°s, and sew through the two 11°s, beam, and two 11°s on the base component. Pick up four 11°s, and sew through the five 11°s at the apex of the Arcos. Repeat these stitches four times. Reinforce and tie a half-hitch knot. Sew through a few more beads to exit the 11° next to the apex 11°.

MAKE EARRINGS

7. Pick up nine 11°s, and sew through the three 11°s at the apex of the Arcos, exiting where you started, to make a loop. Reinforce, and end the thread. Attach a jump ring and earring finding to the loop. Make a second earring to match.

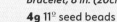

Supplies

Bracelet, 8 in. (20cm)

4g 11° seed beads

4g 8° cylinder beads

20 Es-o beads

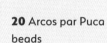

20 three-hole Czech-Mates beam beads

20 Arcos par Puca beads

2 4mm jump rings

Clasp

Earrings
1g 11° seed beads

1g 8° cylinder beads

8 Es-o beads

8 three-hole Czech-Mates beam beads

8 Arcos par Puca beads

2 4mm jump rings

Pair of earring wires

Both projects
Beading needle and thread

2 pairs of chainnose pliers

ORIENTATION

Convex

Concave

FINISH THE BRACELET

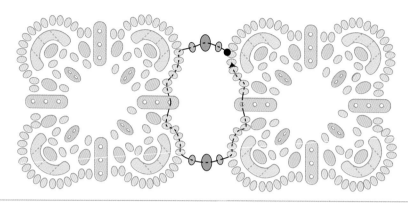

8. Make a total of six more components. Attach the components: Use existing thread or add new thread. Exit the sixth 11º after a beam, pick up an 11º, an 8º, and an 11º, and sew through the sixth 11º before a beam on a second component. Sew through the beadwork along the exterior of the second component to exit the sixth bead after the beam. Pick up an 11º, an 8º, and an 11º, and sew through the sixth 11º before the beam on the first component. Reinforce and end the thread. Repeat to attach the remaining components.

9. To attach a clasp, exit the fourth 11º after a beam. Pick up 13 11ºs, and sew through the four beads before the beam, the beam, and the four beads after the beam. Reinforce, and end the thread. Repeat on the other end of the bracelet. Attach a jump ring and clasp half to each end loop.

STARBURST EARRINGS

Learn a clever way to wrap a crystal and make a pair of earrings at the same time. The StormDuo edging adds the rays needed to make your starburst shine.

MAKE THE EARRINGS

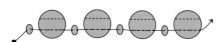

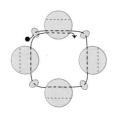

1. Thread a needle on a 50-in. (1.27m) piece of thread, and pick up a repeating pattern of an 11º seed bead and a DiscDuo bead four times.

2. Sew through all of the beads again to make a circle, leaving a 6-in. (15cm) tail. Sew through all of the beads a third time, and tie a half-hitch knot. Sew through all of the beads plus a few extra, and exit a DiscDuo.

NOTE: Tying a knot on each round before and after you switch directions keeps the component solid, even if the hole causes the thread to fray.

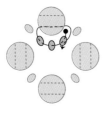

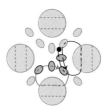
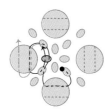

3. Pick up three 11ºs, and sew through the same hole of the DiscDuo you just exited. Sew through the first 11º added. This will be your shared bead.

4. Pick up two 11ºs, and sew through the used hole of the next DiscDuo. Sew through the shared beads and the two 11ºs a third time, and continue through the next DiscDuo. Pick up two 11ºs, and sew through the last 11º added in the previous stitch (the shared bead). Sew through the DiscDuo again and the following 11º. Pick up an 11º, and sew through the third 11º added in step 3. Sew through the DiscDuo again. You should now have a netting around all of the inner holes of the DiscDuo. Exit the DiscDuo, turn, and sew through the open hole of the same DiscDuo.

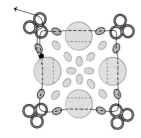

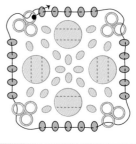

5. Pick up an 11º, a Trinity bead, and an 11º, and sew through the open hole of the next DiscDuo. Repeat this stitch three times. Reinforce, tie half-hitch knot, and exit the Trinity. Turn, and sew through an adjacent open hole on the same Trinity.

6. Pick up five 11ºs, and sew through the corresponding hole on the next Trinity. Repeat three times. Exit the first 11º after a Trinity.

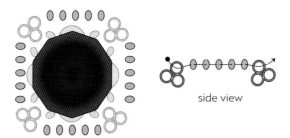

7. Place the crystal in the beadwork so the point is resting on the DiscDuos.

NOTE: Work with the thread in the direction that your arm pulls away from your body. This can be either way, depending on whether you are left-handed or right handed. Work whichever way is most comfortable for you.

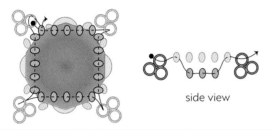

8. Sew through all of the beads you added in the last step. Sew through all the beads again, and exit the first 11° after a Trinity.

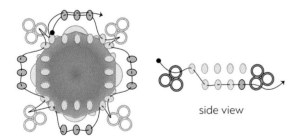

9. Pick up three 11°s, and sew through the 11° before the Trinity, the adjacent hole of the Trinity, and the next 11°. Repeat this stitch three times. Exit the third bead added. (You have only use the first two holes of the Trinity bead at this point.)

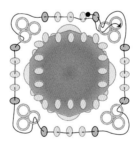
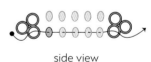

10. Pick up an 11°, and sew through the first hole you used on the Trinity. This will be placed on the bezel cup lower part. Pick up an 11°, and sew through the next set of three 11°s. Repeat this stitch three times. Reinforce, tie a half-hitch knot, and exit the open hole of the Trinity.

NOTE: The more times you can sew through the beads on the outside row using even tension, the sturdier the rays will hold.

Supplies

Earrings

  5g 11° seed beads

  2g 8° seed beads

  8 6x6mm Trinity beads

8 DiscDuo beads

24 StormDuo beads

2 12mm crystal rivolis

2 4mm jump rings

Pair of earring wires

Beading needle and thread

2 pairs of chainnose pliers

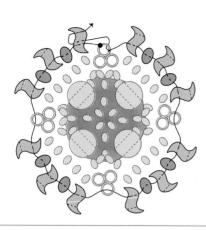

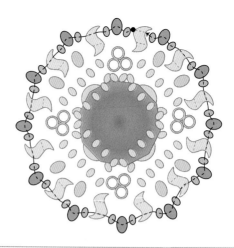

11. Flip the work over. Pick up a StormDuo bead, an 11º, a StormDuo, an 11º, and a StormDuo, and sew through the open hole of the next Trinity. Repeat this stitch three times. Reinforce, tie a knot, and exit the inner side of the StormDuo. Sew through the open hole of the same StormDuo.

12. Flip the work over. Pick up an 11º, an 8º, and an 11º, and sew through the open hole of the next StormDuo. Repeat this stitch 11 times. Reinforce. Tie a knot, and exit an 8º located above a Trinity.

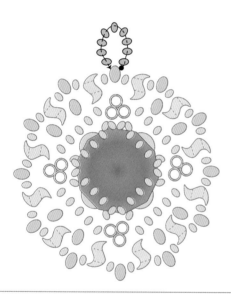

13. Pick up nine 11ºs, and sew through the same 8º the thread is exiting to make a loop. Sew through the loop twice more to reinforce the thread path. Exit into the outer row, and sew through a few beads. Tie a half-hitch knot on the main row after leaving the loop. Sew through the outer row once again, and end the threads.

Attach a jump ring and earring wire to the loop.

Make a second earring.

PATCHWORK BRACELET

This bracelet design is comprised of clearly distinguished shaped beads. Use four types of two-hole beads to achieve this look.

MAKE THE COMPONENTS

1. Thread a needle on a 50-in. (1.27m) piece of thread, and pick up four 11º cylinder beads.

2. Sew through all of the beads again, leaving a 6-in. (15cm) tail.

3. Pick up an 11º seed bead, and sew through the next cylinder. Repeat three times. Sew through all of the beads again, tie a half-hitch knot, and exit the first 11º.

4. Pick up a mini RounDuo bead, and sew through the next 11º. Repeat this stitch three times. Reinforce, exit the last mini RounDuo, turn, and sew through the open hole of the same mini RounDuo.

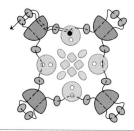

5. Pick up an 11º, a Kos par Puca bead (curved side), and two 11ºs, and sew through the open hole of the Kos again (flat side). Pick up an 11º, and sew through the open hole of the next mini RounDuo. Repeat these stitches three times. Reinforce the round, tie a half-hitch knot, and sew through the second 11º above the Kos (flat side).

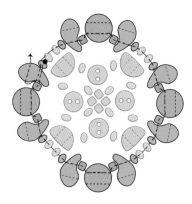

6. Pick up an 11º, a Paisley Duo (lower outer curved side), a cylinder, a DiscDuo, a cylinder, a Paisley Duo (lower inside curve), and an 11º, and sew through the next two 11ºs above the Kos (flat side). Repeat this stitch three times. Reinforce. Exit the first Paisley Duo, turn, and sew through the second hole of the same Paisley Duo.

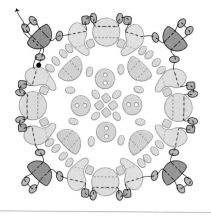

7. Pick up an 11º, a Kos (curved side), and two 11ºs, and sew through the open hole of the same Kos (flat side). Pick up an 11º, and sew through the next Paisley Duo. Pick up a cylinder and an 11º, and sew through the next DiscDuo. Pick up an 11º and a cylinder, and sew through the next Paisley Duo. Repeat these stitches three times. Reinforce well. Exit an 11º above the Kos (flat side).

Make three more components.

FINISH THE BRACELET

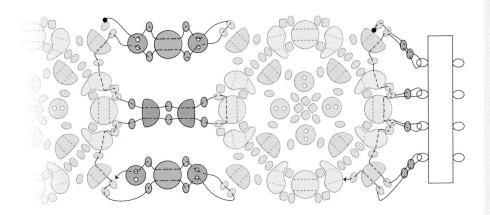

Supplies

Bracelet, 7½ in. (19.1cm)

- **4g** 11º cylinder beads
- **3g** 11º seed beads
- **28** mini RounDuo beads
- **38** Kos par Puca beads
- **32** Paisley Duo beads
- **22** DiscDuo beads
- 4-loop clasp
- Beading needle and thread

NOTE: You can get creative: DiscDuos can be replaced with honeycomb or two-hole cabochons. ZoliDuo beads can be exchanged for Paisley Duos.

ORIENTATION

Flat side   Convex side

Concave side   Convex side

Wide end   Tip end

8. Thread a needle on the tail or add a new thread to one component. Pick up a mini RounDuo, an 11º, a DiscDuo, an 11º, and a mini RounDuo, and sew through the corresponding two 11ºs on a second component and the open hole of the mini RounDuo. Pick up an 11º, and sew through the open hole of the DiscDuo. Pick up an 11º, and sew through the corresponding two 11ºs on the first component. Reinforce, and sew through the beadwork to exit the center 11º before the DiscDuo. Pick up an 11º, a Kos (flat side), an 11º, a Kos (curved side), and an 11º, and sew through the 11º, DiscDuo, and 11º on the second component. Pick up an 11º, and sew through the open hole of the Kos. Pick up an 11º, and sew through the open hole of the next Kos. Pick up an 11º, and sew back into the first component. Reinforce, sew through the beadwork to the lower section, and repeat the first part of this step.

9. At one end of the bracelet, exit the 11º above the Kos (flat side). Pick up two 11ºs, and sew through the first loop on the clasp. Sew back through the two 11ºs and back into the bead you first exited. Reinforce. Sew through the beadwork to the 11º before the DiscDuo. Pick up an 11º, and sew through the second loop of clasp. Sew back through the 11º just added, and reinforce. Repeat these stitches, backwards, to attach the remaining loops on the clasp. Repeat this step to add the other clasp half to the other end of the bracelet. End the threads.

QUATREFOIL BRACELET

This flat piece is similar in construction to the previous Patchwork Bracelet, but uses different bead shapes and embellishment.

MAKE THE COMPONENT

1. Thread a needle on a 50-in. (1.27m) piece of thread, and pick up a repeating pattern of an 11º seed bead and a mini RounDuo bead four times.

Supplies

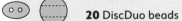

Bracelet, 8 in. (20cm)

○   **4g** 11º seed beads

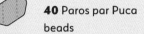   **30** mini RounDuo beads

   20 DiscDuo beads

   40 Paros par Puca beads

   32 Leaf Duo beads

   4-loop clasp

Beading needle and thread

2. Sew through all of the beads a second time to make a circle, leaving a 4-in. (10cm) tail. Reinforce, and tie a half-hitch knot. Sew through all of the beads again, and exit an 11º.

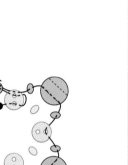

3. Sew through the mini RounDuo, turn, and sew through the other hole of the same mini RounDuo. Pick up an 11º, a DiscDuo bead, and an 11º, and sew through the open hole of the next RounDuo. Repeat this last stitch three times.

Reinforce, tie a half-hitch knot, and exit an 11º after a RounDuo.

ORIENTATION

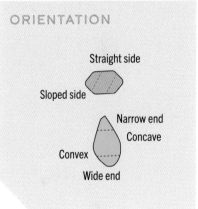

Straight side

Sloped side

Narrow end

Concave

Convex

Wide end

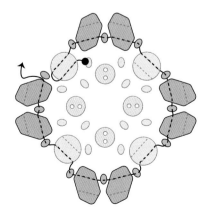

4. Sew through the DiscDuo, turn, and sew through the open hole of the same DiscDuo. Pick up an 11º, a Paros par Puca bead (short slope hole), an 11º, a Paros (straight side hole), and an 11º, and sew through the open hole of the next DiscDuo. Repeat this last stitch three times. Reinforce the row, tie a half-hitch knot, and exit a Paros (straight side).

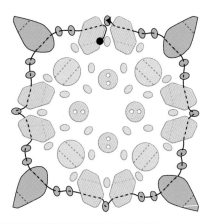

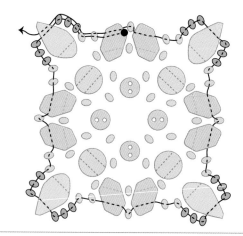

5. Turn and sew through the open hole of the Paros. Pick up two 11ºs, a Leaf Duo bead (wide end, concave), and two 11ºs, and sew through the open hole of the next Paros. Pick up an 11º, and sew through the open hole of the next Paros. Repeat these last two stitches three times. Reinforce the row, and exit the 11º between two Paros.

6. Sew through the Paros and two 11ºs. Pick up three 11ºs, and sew through the open hole of the Leaf Duo. Pick up three 11ºs, and sew through the next two 11ºs, Paros, 11º, and Paros, and two 11ºs. Repeat these last two stitches three times. Reinforce the entire row, tie a half-hitch knot, and exit a Leaf Duo.

Make four more components.

FINISH THE BRACELET

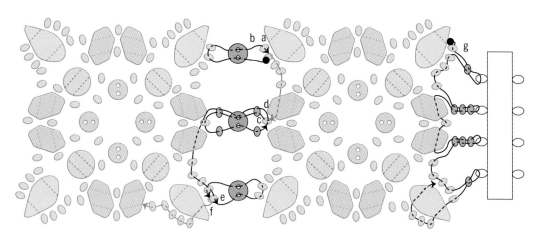

7. **a.** Sew through the first two 11ºs after the Leaf Duo. Pick up a RounDuo, and sew through the two 11ºs on the next component. Sew through the open hole of the RounDuo.
b. Sew through the 11ºs on the first component and exit the 11º after the first Paros.
c. Pick up an 11º, a RounDuo, and an 11º, and sew through the 11º between Paros on the first component. Pick up an 11º, and sew through the open hole of the RounDuo. Pick up an 11º, and sew through the 11º between Paros on the first component.
d. Sew through the beads added in the previous step. Then continue through the exterior beads to exit near the tip of the LeafDuo.
e. Pick up a RounDuo, and sew through the two 11ºs on the other component. Sew through the open hole of the RounDuo, and sew back through the two 11ºs you exited at the start of this step. Reinforce all the connections.
f. End the thread in the component.

8. Attach a new thread on an end component and exit an outer 11º directly after a LeafDuo as shown at **point g**. Pick up an 11º, and sew through the first loop of the clasp. Sew back through the 11º just added. Sew through the next four 11ºs. Pick up three 11ºs, and sew through the second loop of the clasp. Sew back through the 11ºs just added and through the Paros, 11º, and the next Paros. Pick up three 11ºs, and sew through the third loop of the clasp. Sew back through the 11ºs just added and the next four 11ºs. Pick up an 11º, and sew through the final loop of the clasp. Sew back through the 11º just added and also the exterior row of the component. Reinforce the thread path on each loop, and end the thread.

9. Repeat step 8 on the other end of the bracelet to attach the other half of the clasp.

HOLIDAY WREATH EARRINGS

Make a festive design that is
sure to be a seasonal favorite.
The components work up quickly
so you can make it during the
afternoon in colors to complement
your evening outfit.

MAKE THE EARRINGS

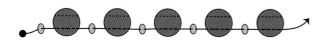

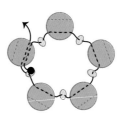

1. Thread a needle on a 50-in. (1.27m) piece of thread, and pick up a repeating pattern of an 11° seed bead and a two-hole cabochon five times.

2. Sew through all of the beads again to make a circle, leaving a 4-in. (10cm) tail. Sew through two more beads, and tie a half-hitch knot. Sew through all the beads plus two more, tie another half-hitch knot, and sew through a few more beads. Exit a two-hole cab.

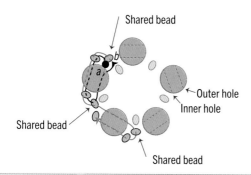

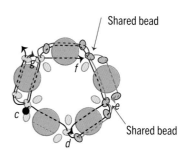

3. a. Pick up two 11°s (the first of these will be the "shared bead"). Turn, and sew through the open hole of the two-hole cab. Pick up two 11°s, and sew through the first hole of the same two-hole cab. (The second bead you pick up will become the shared bead.)

b. Sew through the first two 11°s added, the second hole of the two-hole cab, and the next two 11°s. Exit the shared bead, and sew through the first hole of the next two-hole cab. Pick up two 11°s, and sew through the open hole of the same two-hole cab your thread is exiting.

4. c. Sew through the two 11°s, the first hole of the next two-hole cab, and the first (shared) bead after it.

d. Pick up an 11°, and sew through the open hole of the two-hole cab. Pick up two 11°s, and sew through the first hole of the two-hole cab, the "shared" 11°, the 11° just added, the second hole of the two-hole cab, and the two 11°s just added. (The second of these is the "shared" bead.)

e. Sew through the first hole of the next two-hole cab, pick up two 11°s, and sew through the open hole of the same two-hole cab. Pick up an 11°, and sew through the "shared" bead, the first hole of the two-hole cab, and the first 11° just added. This is a shared bead.

f. Pick up an 11°, and sew through the open hole of the next two-hole cab. Pick up an 11°, and sew through the very first shared bead you added in step 3. Sew through the inner hole of the same two-hole cab, the two 11°s, the outer hole of the same two-hole cab and the first 11°. Sew through the very first shared bead you added in step 3.

g. Pass through the first (inner) hole of the very first two-hole cab, both 11°s, the outer hole of the two-hole cab, the 11°, and the shared 11°, and then continue into the first (inner) hole and the two 11°s and the outer hole of the same two-hole cab and the 11° after it.

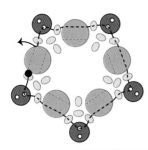

Supplies

Earrings

4g 11º seed beads

10 two-hole cabochons

10 mini RounDuo beads

10 EVA beads

20 Czech button beads

Pair of earring wires

Beading needle and thread

2 pair of chainnose pliers

ORIENTATION

Tip end

Wide end

5. Exit the 11º, pick up a mini RounDuo, and sew through the next 11º, two-hole cab, and 11º. Repeat this stitch four times. Sew through all of the beads just added again, and exit the 11º after a mini RounDuo.

6. Pick up an 11º, an EVA bead (inside hole), and six 11ºs, and sew through the open outer hole of the EVA. Pick up an 11º, and sew through the next 11º, mini RounDuo, and 11º. Repeat these stitches four times. Sew through the entire round again, and exit the mini RounDuo.

7. Sew through two 11ºs, the first side of the EVA, and the six 11ºs. Pick up an 11º, a Czech button bead, and an 11º, and sew through the open hole of the mini RounDuo. Pick up an 11º, a button, and an 11º, and sew through the six 11ºs at the peak of the EVA. Repeat these stitches four times. Sew through all of the beads just added, and exit the third 11º above the EVA peak.

8. Pick up nine 11ºs, and sew through the two 11ºs at the top of the peak. Reinforce the entire loop, and end the threads. Attach an earring finding to the loop. Repeat to make a second earring.

SAND DOLLAR EARRINGS

Weave seed beads into four-hole beads to make a netted style component. This cute-as-a-button component resembles sand dollars—light and airy, it's perfect for summery beach style.

MAKE THE EARRINGS

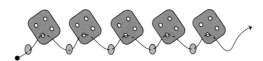

1. Thread a needle on a 60-in. (1.52m) piece of thread, and pick up a repeating pattern of an 11º seed bead and a QuadraTile bead five times.

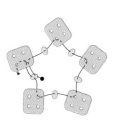

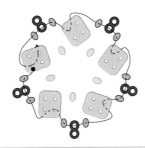

Earrings

○ **1g** 11º seed beads

◯ **1g** 8º seed beads

 10 DiscDuo beads

 10 2x5mm Infinity beads

 10 QuadraTile beads

 2 6mm drop beads

Pair of earring wires

2 4mm jump rings

Beading needle and thread

2 pair of chainnose pliers

2. Sew through all the beads again to make a circle, leaving a 5-in. (13cm) tail. Sew through all of the beads again, tie a half-hitch knot, and sew through all of the beads again, exiting a QuadraTile. Turn, and sew through the adjacent (second) hole of the same QuadraTile.

3. Pick up an 11º, an Infinity bead, and an 11º, and sew through the corresponding second hole of the next QuadraTile. Repeat this stitch four times. Sew through all of the beads in the row again, tie a half-hitch knot, and exit a QuadraTile. Turn, and sew through the adjacent (third) hole on the opposite side of the same QuadraTile.

ORIENTATION

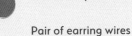

Hole 4

Hole 2   Hole 3

Hole 1

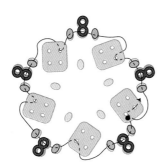

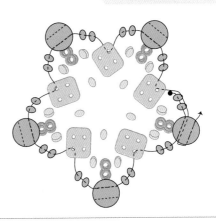

4. Flip the beadwork over. Pick up an 11º, an Infinity bead, and an 11º, and sew through the corresponding third hole of the next QuadraTile. Repeat this stitch four times. Reinforce, tie a half-hitch knot, and exit a QuadraTile. Turn, and sew through the open (fourth) hole of the same QuadraTile.

5. Pick up two 11ºs, a DiscDuo bead, and two 11ºs, and sew through the open hole of the next QuadraTile. Repeat this stitch four times. Reinforce the row, exit the DiscDuo, turn, and sew through the open hole of the same DiscDuo.

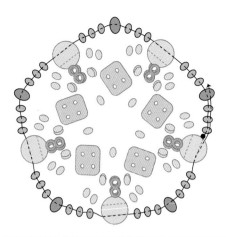

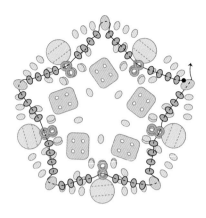

6. Pick up three 11⁰s, an 8⁰, and three 11⁰s, and sew through open hole of the next DiscDuo. Repeat this stitch four times. Reinforce the row, and exit an 8⁰.

7. Pick up four 11⁰s (shown in green for clarity), and sew through the open hole of the Infinity (pulling away from your body—see the note, below). Pick up four 11⁰s, and sew through the next 8⁰ in the outer row. Repeat these stitches four times.

NOTE: You can work on either side of the pendant, depending on which side of the hole you sew through. One way will have you pulling thread away from your body, resulting in good tension and comfortable arm motion. The other side will require you to pull thread toward your body. This will make it more difficult to control tension.

FINISH THE EARRINGS

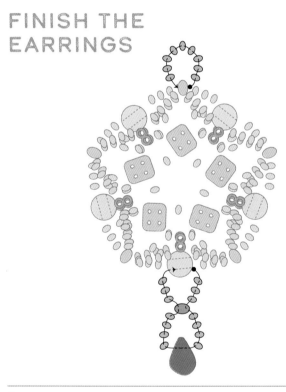

8. Flip the beadwork over. Pick up four 11⁰s, and sew through the open hole of the Infinity. Pick up four 11⁰s, and sew through the next 8⁰. Repeat these stitches four times. Reinforce.

9. Make a loop: With the thread exiting an 8⁰, pick up nine 11⁰s, and pass through the same 8⁰ on the opposite side. Reinforce twice. End the thread.

10. Add a drop: Add new thread, if needed. Exit the outer hole of the DiscDuo opposite the loop, pick up three 11⁰s, an 8⁰, four 11⁰s, a drop, and four 11⁰s, and sew through the 8⁰. Pick up three 11⁰s and sew back through the same hole of the DiscDuo. Reinforce, and end the thread. Repeat to make a second earring

STAR BRIGHT PENDANT

A festive star shape shines bright in a pendant (or an ornament!). Using geometric beads results in a great pointed triangle look.

MAKE THE PENDANT

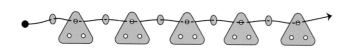

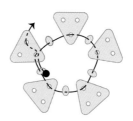

1. Thread a needle on a 50-in. (1.27m) piece of thread, and pick up a repeating pattern of an 11º seed bead and an eMMA bead five times.

2. Sew through all of the beads again to make a circle, leaving a 4-in. (10cm) tail. Sew through all the beads two more times, tying half-hitch knots. Exit an eMMA. Turn, and sew through the second hole of the same eMMA.

NOTE: By making so many thread passes at this point, you have created a tight core for your component.

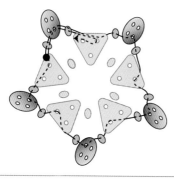

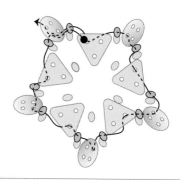

3. Pick up an 11º, a QuadraLentil, and an 11º, and sew through the second hole of the next eMMA. Repeat this stitch four times. Retrace the thread path through all of the beads just added twice, tying half-hitch knots, and exit an eMMA. Turn, and sew through the open hole of the same eMMA.

4. Pick up an 11º, and sew through the second hole of the QuadraLentil. Pick up an 11º, and sew through the open hole of the eMMA. Repeat this stich four times. Sew through all the beads in this round two more times, tying a few half-hitch knots, and exit a QuadraLentil. Sew through the third hole of the same QuadraLentil, and end the tail.

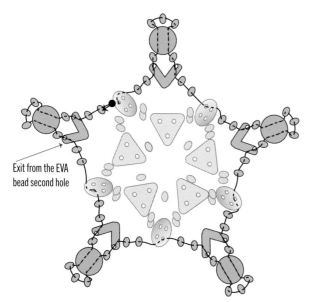

Exit from the EVA bead second hole

5. Pick up two 11ºs, an EVA bead (outside hole), an 11º, a DiscDuo, and three 11ºs, and sew through the open hole of the DiscDuo. Pick up an 11º, and sew through the open hole of the EVA. Pick up two 11ºs, and sew through the third hole of the next QuadraLentil. Repeat these stitches three times. Sew through the first nine beads added in this step (the first arm), and exit the second side of the EVA.

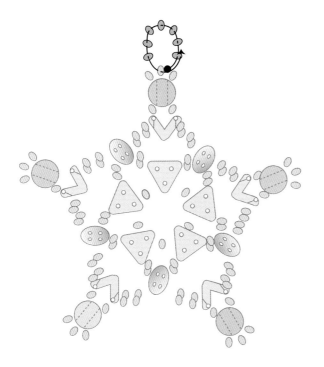

Supplies

Pendant

 1g 11° seed beads

 5 eMMA beads

 5 QuadraLentil beads

 5 DiscDuo beads

5 EVA beads

Beading needle and thread

ORIENTATION

Hole 3   Hole 2

Hole 1

Hole 4

Hole 3   Hole 1

Hole 2

6. Pick up two 11°s, and sew through the open hole of the QuadraLentil. Pick up two 11°s, and sew through the next seven beads in the following arm, exiting the second hole of the EVA. Repeat these stitches four times, and exit the second 11° in the three-bead set above the DiscDuo.

7. Pick up seven 11°s, and sew through the 11° the thread is exiting. Reinforce twice, and sew back into the beadwork. Sew through the exterior beads you added in step 6 to tighten them up, tying several half-hitch knots along the way, and end the thread. Attach a neck wire (or ornament hook!) to the loop to hang.

NOTE: The final reinforcing will help tighten the beadwork and keep the arms firm.

ASTERIA PENDANT

This statement-making pendant uses three- and four-hole beads along with seed beads. At just under two inches wide, two components make for a stunning pair of earrings, too.

MAKE THE PENDANT

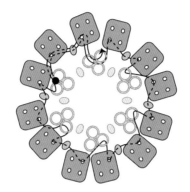

1. Thread a needle on a 60-in. (1.52m) piece of thread, and pick up a repeating pattern of an 11º seed bead and a Trinity bead six times.

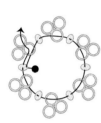

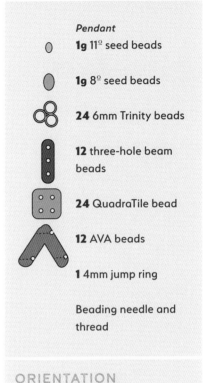

Supplies

Pendant

○ **1g** 11º seed beads

● **1g** 8º seed beads

24 6mm Trinity beads

12 three-hole beam beads

24 QuadraTile bead

12 AVA beads

1 4mm jump ring

Beading needle and thread

ORIENTATION

Hole 1
Hole 2
Hole 3

Hole 4 · Hole 3
Hole 1 · Hole 2

Hole 3
Hole 1 · Hole 2

Hole 4 · Hole 3
Hole 1 · Hole 2

Hole 2 · Hole 3
Hole 1

figure a

2. Sew through all of the beads again, leaving a 6-in. (15cm) tail. Sew through all the beads a third time, and tie a half-hitch knot. Exit a Trinity, turn, and sew through an adjacent hole of the same Trinity.

3. Pick up a QuadraTile bead, an 11º, and a QuadraTile, and sew through the corresponding open hole on the next Trinity. Repeat this stitch five times. Sew through all the beads again plus three, and tie a half-hitch knot. Sew through a few more beads to exit a Trinity, and sew through the adjacent (second) hole of the same QuadraTile. Pull your thread away from your body when stitching. (**Figure a** shows side view.)

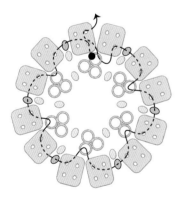

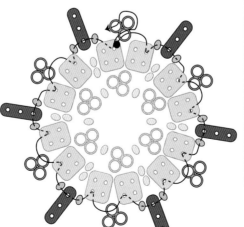

4. Pick up an 11º, and sew through the second hole of the next QuadraTile and the open hole of the next Trinity. Repeat this stitch three times. Turn, and sew through the third hole of a QuadraTile before a Trinity. (**Figure a** shows side view.)

5. Pick up a Trinity, and sew through the corresponding hole of the next QuadraTile. Pick up an 11º, a beam bead (end hole), and an 11º, and sew through the corresponding hole of the next QuadraTile. Repeat these stitches five times, reinforce, and exit a Trinity. Turn, and sew through the second hole of the same Trinity.

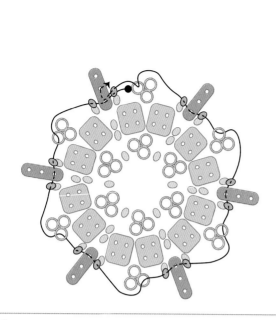

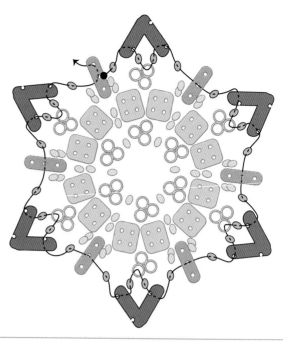

6. Flip the beadwork over. Pick up an 11º, and sew through the other end hole of the beam. Pick up an 11º, and sew through the open (fourth) hole of the next QuadraTile. Repeat these stitches five times. Exit a beam, and sew through the middle hole of the same beam.

7. Pick up an 11º, an AVA (leg, from the outside), and an 11º, and sew through the open hole of the next Trinity. Pick up an 11º, sew through the second hole of AVA, pick up an 11º, and sew through the middle hole of the next beam. Repeat these stitches five times. Reinforce as you are able. Tie a knot, exit a beam, turn, and sew through the open hole of the same beam.

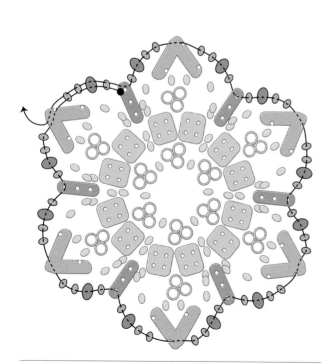

8. Pick up an 11º, an 8º, and two 11ºs, and sew through the open hole of the AVA. Pick up two 11ºs, an 8º, and an 11º, and sew through the open hole of the next beam. Repeat these stitches five times. Reinforce, and exit an AVA.

9. Pick up nine 11ºs, and sew through the same hole of the AVA. Reinforce, and end the thread. Attach a jump ring to the loop.

CARNIVAL EARRINGS

These glimmering, glittery earrings remind me of a celebration—like a carnival on a hot summer's day.

MAKE THE EARRINGS

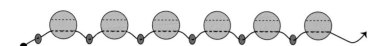

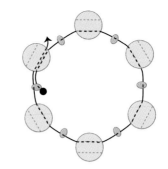

1. Thread a needle on a 50-in. (1.27m) piece of thread, and pick up a repeating pattern of an 11º seed bead and a DiscDuo bead six times.

2. Sew through all of the beads again to make a circle, leaving a 6-in. (15cm) tail. Tie a half-hitch knot, and sew through all of the beads again, exiting a DiscDuo.

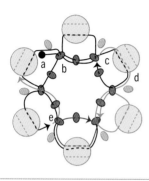

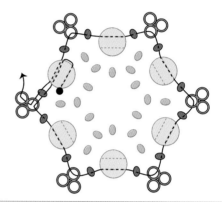

3. a. Pick up three 11ºs (the first and third beads will be "shared" beads), and sew through the same hole of the DiscDuo and through the first shared bead.
b. Pick up two 11ºs (the second will become a shared bead), and sew through the next DiscDuo, the first shared bead, and the two 11ºs just added.
c. Sew through the next DiscDuo, pick up two 11ºs, and sew through the shared bead and the same DiscDuo.
d. Repeat these stitches to complete the round.
e. Sew through the next three shared beads.

4. Sew through the DiscDuo, turn, and continue through the open hole of the same DiscDuo. Pick up an 11º, a Trinity bead, and an 11º, and sew through the open hole of the next DiscDuo. Repeat these stitches five times. Exit a Trinity, turn, and continue through the adjacent (second) hole of the same Trinity.

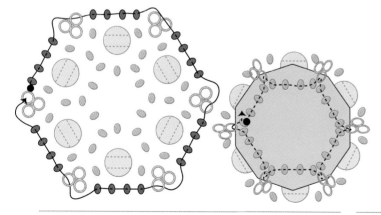

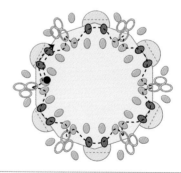

5. Pick up four 11ºs, and sew through the corresponding hole of the next Trinity. Repeat this stitch five times (keep the tension loose). When all the beads are added, place the rivoli in the space. Pull the beadwork tight, and sew through the beads just added again. Exit the first 11º after a Trinity.

6. Pick up two 11ºs, and sew into the 11º before the next Trinity, the Trinity and the 11º after it. Repeat this stitch five times. Exit the first set of two 11ºs just added.

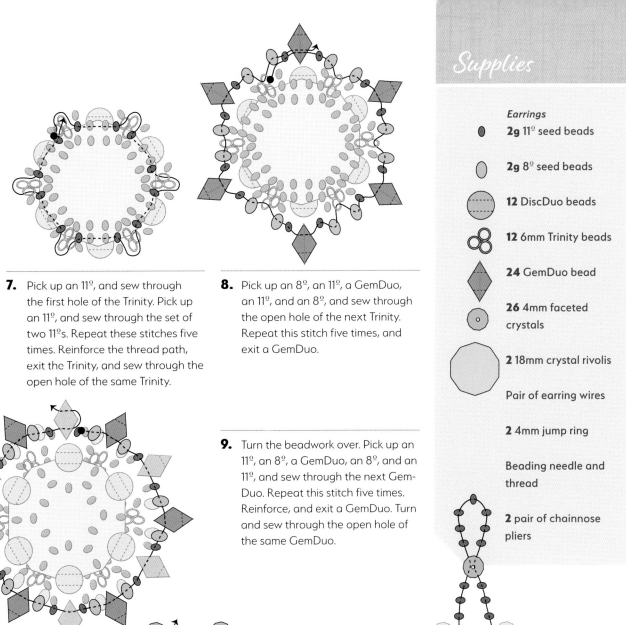

7. Pick up an 11º, and sew through the first hole of the Trinity. Pick up an 11º, and sew through the set of two 11ºs. Repeat these stitches five times. Reinforce the thread path, exit the Trinity, and sew through the open hole of the same Trinity.

8. Pick up an 8º, an 11º, a GemDuo, an 11º, and an 8º, and sew through the open hole of the next Trinity. Repeat this stitch five times, and exit a GemDuo.

9. Turn the beadwork over. Pick up an 11º, an 8º, a GemDuo, an 8º, and an 11º, and sew through the next Gem-Duo. Repeat this stitch five times. Reinforce, and exit a GemDuo. Turn and sew through the open hole of the same GemDuo.

Earrings

● **2g** 11º seed beads

○ **2g** 8º seed beads

◯ **12** DiscDuo beads

◉◉ **12** 6mm Trinity beads

◆ **24** GemDuo bead

● **26** 4mm faceted crystals

◯ **2** 18mm crystal rivolis

Pair of earring wires

2 4mm jump ring

Beading needle and thread

2 pair of chainnose pliers

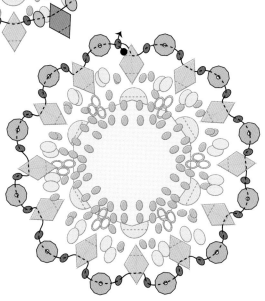

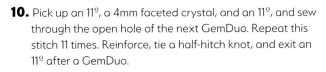

10. Pick up an 11º, a 4mm faceted crystal, and an 11º, and sew through the open hole of the next GemDuo. Repeat this stitch 11 times. Reinforce, tie a half-hitch knot, and exit an 11º after a GemDuo.

11. Pick up three 11ºs, a crystal, and seven 11ºs, and sew back through the crystal. Pick up three 11ºs, and sew into the 11º before the GemDuo. Reinforce, and end the thread. Attach an earring wire to the bead loop with a jump ring. Repeat to make a second earring.

SPROCKET PENDANT

A cleverly constructed piece, this design looks quite fancy. Two sizes of Infinity beads are interspersed with different colors of two-hole cabochons (or honeycomb or DiscDuo beads, if you like).

MAKE THE PENDANT

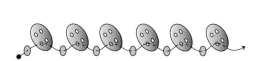

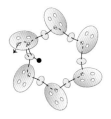

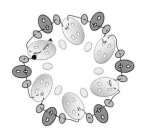

1. Thread a needle on a 70-in. (1.78m) piece of thread, and pick up a repeating pattern of an 11º seed bead and a QuadraLentil bead six times.

2. Sew through all of the beads again to make a circle. Tie a half-hitch knot, sew through all of the beads again, and exit the QuadraLentil. Turn, and sew through the adjacent (second) hole of the same QuadraLentil.

3. Pick up an 11º, an Es-o bead, and an 11º, and sew through the corresponding second hole of the next QuadraLentil. Repeat this stitch five times. Exit the QuadraLentil, turn, and sew through the opposite (third) hole of the same QuadraLentil.

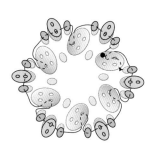

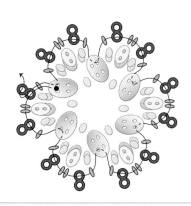

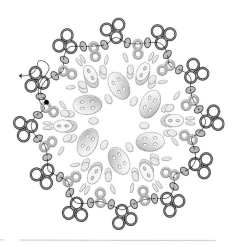

4. Flip the beadwork over. Pick up an 11º, an Es-o (shown in green for clarity), and an 11º, and sew through the corresponding third hole of the next QuadraLentil. Repeat this stitch five times. Exit the QuadraLentil, turn, and sew through the open (fourth) hole of the same QuadraLentil.

5. Pick up an 11º Demi bead, a 2x5mm (small) Infinity bead, two Demis, a small Infinity, and a Demi, and sew through the open hole of the next QuadraLentil. Repeat this stitch five times. Reinforce the row. (These beads will look wonky.) Exit an Infinity before the two Demis. Turn, and sew through the second hole of the same Infinity.

6. Pick up an 11º, a Trinity bead, and an 11º, and sew through the open hole of the next Infinity. Repeat this stitch 11 times. Reinforce. (The beads will still be a little wonky.) Exit the Trinity, turn, and sew through the far (second) hole of the same Trinity.

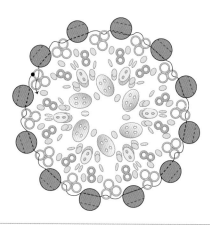

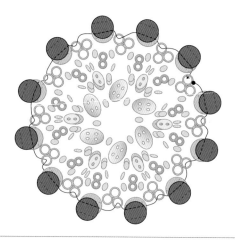

7. Pick up a two-hole cabochon, flat side facing the open hole of Trinity, and sew through the corresponding hole of the next Trinity. Repeat this stitch 11 times. Make sure all of the flat sides of the cabs are facing the open hole of the Trinity, exit a Trinity, and sew through the open hole of the same bead.

8. Flip the beadwork over. Pick up a two-hole cab, and sew through the open hole of the next Trinity. Make sure all flat sides of the two-hole cabs are facing the flat sides of the cabs added in step 7. Repeat this stitch 11 times. Exit the Trinity.

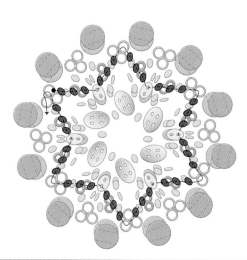

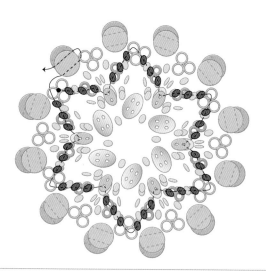

9. Pick up three 11⁰s (shown in pink for clarity), and sew through the open hole of the Es-o on the same side of the beadwork as the two-hole cab. Pick up three 11⁰s, and sew through the third hole of the next Trinity. Repeat these stitches five times. Exit a Trinity, and sew through the second hole of the Trinity.

10. Flip the beadwork over. Pick up three 11⁰s, and sew through the open hole of the Es-o. Pick up three 11⁰s, and sew through the second hole of the next Trinity. Repeat these stitches five times. Exit a Trinity, and sew through the open hole of a two-hole cab.

11. Pick up an 11º, a 3x6mm (large) Infinity bead, and an 11º, and sew through the open hole of the next two-hole cab. Repeat this stitch 11 times. Reinforce, exit a large Infinity, turn, and sew through the open hole of the same Infinity.

12. Flip the beadwork over. Pick up an 11º, and sew through the open hole of the next two-hole cab. Pick up an 11º, and sew through the open hole of the next Infinity. Repeat these stitches 11 times. Reinforce the row, and exit the Infinity.

13. Add a bail: Pick up nine 11ºs, and sew through the second hole of the Infinity on the same side of the bead the thread is exiting. Pick up two 11ºs, and sew through the middle five existing 11ºs (skipping the first two beads in the loop). Pick up two 11ºs, and sew through the Infinity using the other hole on the same side of the bead. Reinforce the thread path a couple of times, and end the threads.

Supplies

Pendant

4g 11º seed beads

1g 11º Demi round beads

2g 8º seed beads

12 6x6mm Trinity beads

24 2x5mm Infinity beads (small)

12 3x6mm Infinity beads (large)

6 QuadraLentil beads

12 4mm mini Es-o beads

24 6mm two-hole cabochons

Beading needle and thread

ORIENTATION

Hole 4

Hole 3   Hole 2

Hole 1

LANTERN EARRINGS

Open-weave beaded beads are the
focal point of these lantern earrings.
String these beaded beads with pearls
to create a necklace, if you like.

MAKE THE BEADED BEAD

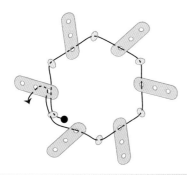

1. Thread a needle on a 50-in. (1.27m) piece of thread, and pick up a repeating pattern of an 11º seed bead and a three-hole beam bead (end hole) six times.

Supplies

Earrings

 3g 11º seed beads

 2g 8º seed beads

 12 8mm Trinity beads

 24 CzechMates three-hole beam beads

12 4mm faceted round beads

2 3-in. (7.6cm) headpins

2 6mm pearls

Pair of earring wires

Beading needle and thread

2 pair of chainnose pliers and wire cutters

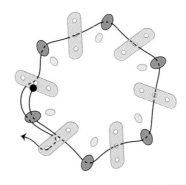

2. Sew through all of the beads a second time to make a circle, leaving a 4-in. (10cm) tail. Sew through two beads, and tie a half-hitch knot. Sew through all of the beads plus two, and tie a half-hitch knot. Sew through a few more beads, and exit a beam. Turn, and sew through the center hole of the same beam.

3. Pick up an 8º seed bead, and sew through the center hole of the next beam. Repeat this stitch five times. Sew through the entire round again, and tie a half-hitch knot. Sew through a few more beads to exit the next beam. Turn, and sew through the open hole of the same beam.

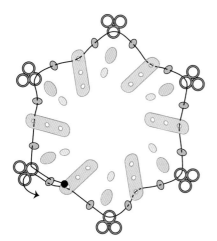

4. Pick up an 11º, a Trinity bead, and an 11º, and sew through the open hole of the next beam. Repeat this stitch five times. Sew through all the beads, and tie a half-hitch knot. Sew through a few more beads, and exit a Trinity. Turn, and sew through the adjacent (second) hole of the Trinity.

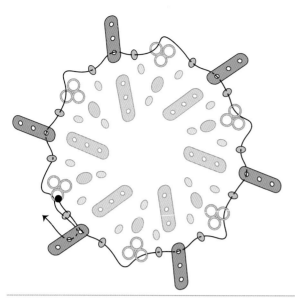

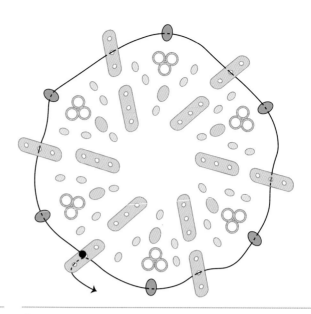

5. Pick up an 11º, a beam, and an 11º, and sew through the second hole of the next Trinity. Repeat this stitch five times. Sew through the entire row plus two, and tie a half-hitch knot. Exit a beam, turn, and sew through the center hole of the same beam.

6. Pick up an 8º, and sew through the second hole of the next beam. Repeat this stitch five times. Sew through the entire row, and tie a half-hitch knot. Turn, and sew through the open hole of the same beam.

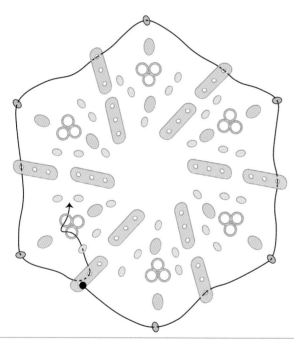

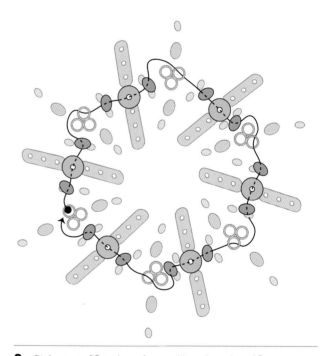

7. Pick up an 11º, and sew through the open hole of the next beam. Repeat this stitch five times. Sew through the entire row, and tie a half-hitch knot. Exit a Trinity.

8. Pick up an 8º, a 4mm faceted bead, and an 8º, and sew through the open hole of the next Trinity. Repeat this stitch five times. Sew through the entire row plus two, and tie a half-hitch knot. Reinforce and end the thread. Make a second beaded bead.

FINISH THE EARRINGS

9. String an 8º, a 6mm pearl, a beaded bead, a 6mm pearl, and an 8º on a headpin, and make a wrapped loop. Connect an earring wire to the loop. Repeat to make a second earring.

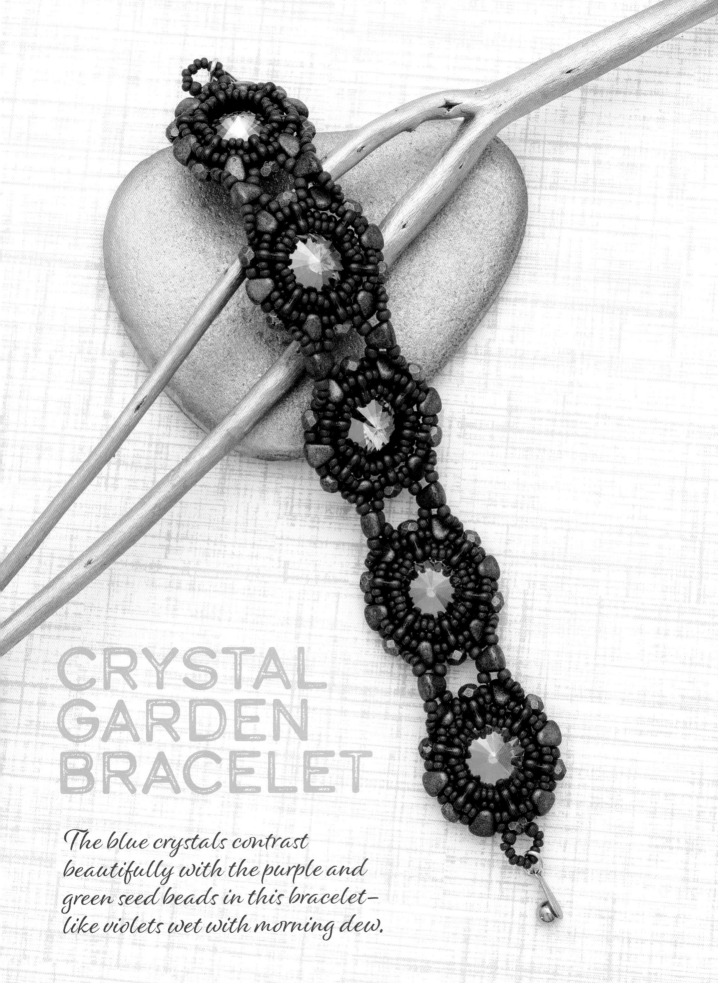

CRYSTAL
GARDEN
BRACELET

*The blue crystals contrast
beautifully with the purple and
green seed beads in this bracelet—
like violets wet with morning dew.*

MAKE THE COMPONENT

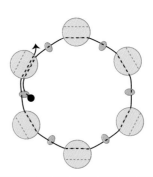

1. Thread a needle on a 50-in. (1.27m) piece of thread, and pick up a repeating pattern of an 11º and a DiscDuo bead six times.

2. Sew through all of the beads again to make a circle. Tie a half-hitch knot, and reinforce. Exit a DiscDuo.

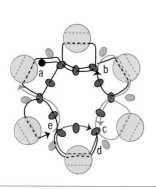

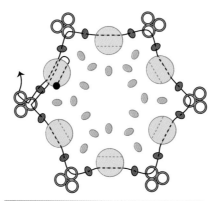

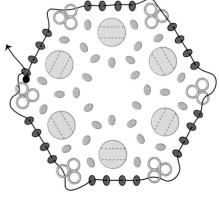

3. a. Pick up three 11ºs (the first and third beads will be "shared" beads), and sew through the same hole of the DiscDuo and the first shared bead. Pick up two 11ºs (the second will become a shared bead). Sew through the next DiscDuo, the first shared bead, and the two 11ºs.
b. Sew through the next DiscDuo, pick up two 11ºs, and sew through the shared bead and the DiscDuo.
c. Repeat these stitches.
d. Repeat these stitches.
e. Sew through the next three shared beads.

4. Sew through a DiscDuo, turn, and sew through the open hole of the same DiscDuo. Pick up an 11º, a Trinity bead, and an 11º, and sew through the open hole of the next DiscDuo. Repeat this stitch five times. Exit a Trinity, turn, and sew through the adjacent (second) hole of the same Trinity.

5. Pick up four 11ºs, and sew through the corresponding hole of the next Trinity. Repeat this stitch five times (keep the tension loose). When all the beads are added, place the rivoli in the space. Pull the beadwork tight, and sew through the beads again, exiting the first 11º after a Trinity.

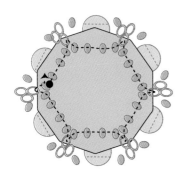

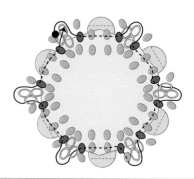

6. Pick up two 11ºs, and sew through the 11º before the next Trinity, the Trinity and the 11º after it. Repeat this stitch five times, and exit the first set of two 11ºs just added.

7. Pick up an 11º, and sew through the first hole of the Trinity. Pick up an 11º, and sew through the set of two 11ºs. Repeat these stitches five times. Reinforce the thread path, exit a Trinity, turn, and sew through the open hole of the same Trinity.

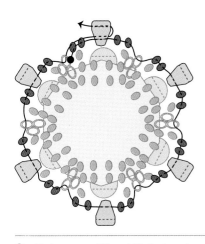

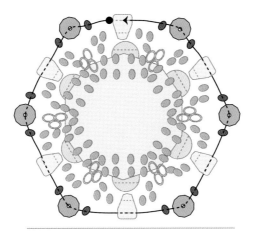

Supplies

Bracelet, 7½ in. (19.1cm)

- **5g** 11º seed beads
- **3g** 8º seed beads
- **30** DiscDuo beads
- **30** 6x6mm Trinity beads
- **38** Nib Bit beads
- **30** 4mm faceted round beads
- **5** 18mm crystal rivolis
- Clasp
- **2** 4mm jump rings
- Beading needle and thread
- **2** pairs of chainnose pliers

8. Pick up two 11ºs, a Nib Bit bead (small end), and two 11ºs, and sew through the open hole of the next Trinity. Repeat this stitch five times, reinforce, exit the Nib Bit, turn, and sew through the open hole of the same Nib Bit.

9. Pick up an 11º, a 4mm faceted round bead, and an 11º, and sew through the open hole of the next Nib Bit. Repeat this stitch five times. Reinforce, tie a half-hitch knot, and exit the Nib Bit.

Make four more components.

FINISH THE BRACELET

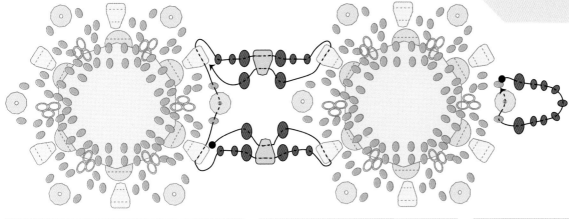

10. Thread a needle on the working thread of a component (exiting a Nib Bit). Pick up an 8º seed bead, a Nib Bit (small end), and an 8º, and sew through the outer hole of a Nib Bit on another component. Pick up two 11ºs and an 8º, and sew through the open hole of the Nib Bit. Pick up an 8º and two 11ºs, and sew through the second Nib Bit on the first component.

11. Sew through the exterior row of beads on the first component, and exit the next Nib Bit. Pick up two 11ºs, an 8º, a Nib Bit (wide end), an 8º, and two 11ºs, and sew through the corresponding Nib Bit on the second component. Pick up an 8º, and sew through the open hole of the Nib Bit. Pick up an 8º, and sew through the Nib Bit on the first component. Reinforce well. Connect all five componets together. End the threads.

12. Attach a comfortable length of thread on an end component, and exit an 11º after a faceted round. Pick up an 8º, seven 11ºs, and an 8º, and sew through the 11º before the faceted round. Reinforce the thread path, and end the thread. Attach a clasp half with a jump ring. Repeat on the other end of the bracelet.

DEW DROPS BRACELET

A solid, circular component is perfect for a sturdy bracelet or a pair of earrings. This design is simply filled with texture.

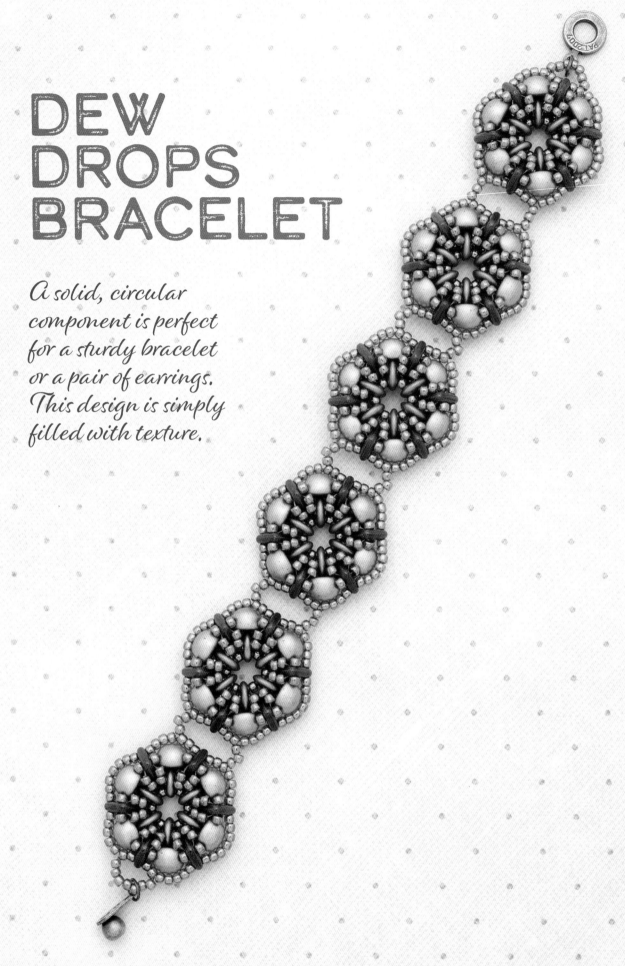

MAKE THE COMPONENT

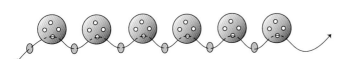

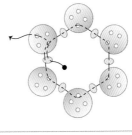

1. Thread a needle on a 50-in. (1.27m) piece of thread, and pick up a repeating pattern of an 11º seed bead and a QuadraLentil bead six times.

2. Sew through all of the beads again to make a circle, leaving a 6-in. (15cm) tail. Tie a half-hitch knot, sew through all the beads again, and exit a QuadraLentil. Turn, and sew through the hole in the same QuadraLentil opposite from where you're working now (second hole).

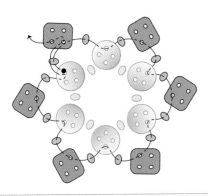

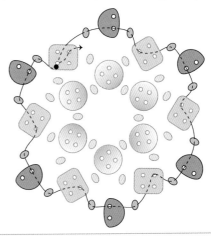

3. Pick up an 11º, a QuadraTile bead, and an 11º, and sew through the corresponding hole of the next Quadra-Lentil. Repeat this stitch five times. Sew through all of the beads to reinforce, and exit the QuadraTile. Turn, and sew through the adjacent (second) hole of the same QuadraTile.

4. Pick up an 11º, a two-hole cabochon, and an 11º, and sew through the corresponding hole of the next QuadraTile. Repeat this stitch five times. Sew through all of the beads again, and exit a QuadraTile. Turn, and sew through the adjacent (third) hole of the QuadraTile.

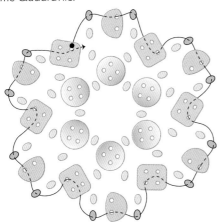

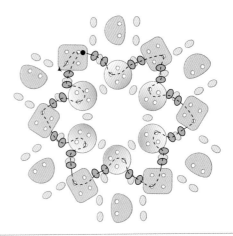

5. Pick up an 11º, and sew through the second hole of the two-hole cab. Pick up an 11º, and sew through the corresponding hole of the QuadraTile. Repeat these stitches five times. Exit a hole of the QuadraTile.

6. Pick up two 11ºs (shown in green for clarity), and sew through the open hole of the QuadraLentil on the same side of the beadwork. Pick up two 11ºs, and sew through the third hole of the next QuadraTile. Repeat these stitches five times. Exit the QuadraTile, turn, and sew through the second hole of the same QuadraTile.

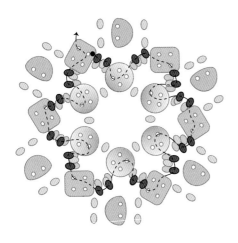

7. Flip the beadwork over. Pick up two 11°s, and sew through the open hole of the QuadraLentil. Pick up two 11°s, and sew through the second hole of the next QuadraTile. Repeat these stitches five times. Exit the QuadraTile, and sew through the fourth hole of the same QuadraTile.

8. Pick up seven 11°s, and sew through the corresponding hole of the next QuadraTile. Repeat this stitch five times. Exit the center 11° on one of the sets on the last row added (the outer row surrounding the two-hole cab).

Make five more components.

Supplies

O O O		**Bracelet, 7½ in. (19.1cm)**
		5g 11° seed beads
		3g 8° seed beads
		36 QuadraLentil beads
		36 QuadraTile beads
		36 two-hole cabo-chons
		Clasp
		2 4mm jump rings
		Beading needle and thread
		2 pair of chainnose pliers

ORIENTATION

Hole 2
Hole 4 — Hole 3
Hole 1

Hole 4
Hole 3 — Hole 2
Hole 1

FINISH THE BRACELET

9. Thread a needle on the working thread of a component (exiting a center 11°). Pick up an 11°, an 8°, and an 11°, and sew through the center bead on the last row added on another component. Sew back through the 11°, 8°, and 11° three-bead set, and continue into the center bead on the first component. Reinforce. Sew through the beadwork to exit the lower half of component. Repeat this step. End the threads.

10. Exit the third 11° before a QuadraTile. Pick up seven 11°s, and sew through the third 11° after the QuadraTile. Sew through the beadwork as shown. Reinforce the thread path, and end the thread. Attach a clasp half with a jump ring. Repeat on the other end of the bracelet.

FIVE-STAR BRACELET

An attention-grabbing design uses back-lit cabochons accented with two-hole cabs for added shimmer. Each component can easily be made into a pendant or a pair of earrings.

MAKE THE BRACELET

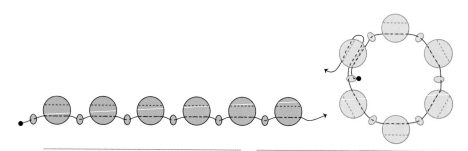 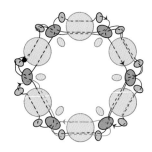

1. Thread a needle on a 60-in. (1.52m) piece of thread, and pick up a repeating pattern of an 11º seed bead and a DiscDuo bead six times.

2. Sew through all of the beads again, leaving a 4-in. (10cm) tail. Tie a half-hitch knot, reinforce, and exit a DiscDuo. Turn, and sew through the open hole of the same DiscDuo.

3. The 8º seed bead in this step is the "shared bead." Pick up an 11º and an 8º, and sew through the first hole of the DiscDuo. * Pick up an 8º and an 11º, and sew through the second hole of the same DiscDuo, the next 11º, and the shared 8º. Sew through the previous hole of the next DiscDuo. Repeat from the asterisk to complete the round.

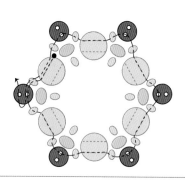 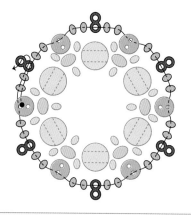 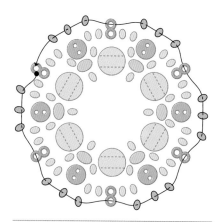

4. Exit an 11º after a DiscDuo. Pick up a mini RounDuo, and sew through the next 11º, DiscDuo, and 11º three-bead set. Repeat this stitch five times. Reinforce, exit the mini RounDuo, turn, and sew through the open hole of the same mini RounDuo.

5. Pick up two 11ºs, an Infinity bead, and two 11ºs, and sew through the open hole of the next mini RounDuo. Repeat this step five times, reinforce, and exit the Infinity. Turn, and sew through the open hole of the same Infinity.

6. Pick up three 11ºs, and sew through the open hole of the next Infinity. Repeat this stitch five times. Do not pull your thread tightly; these beads will get pulled into the center to hold the cabochon in place.

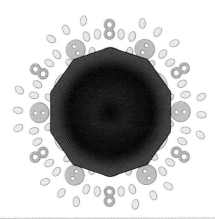

Bracelet, 7½ in. (19.1cm)

5g 11º seed beads

3g 8º seed beads

30 6mm DiscDuo beads

38 4mm mini RounDuo beads

30 mini Infinity beads

30 two-hole cabochons

5 18mm back-lit cabochons

Clasp

2 4mm jump rings

Beading needle and thread

2 pairs of chainnose pliers

7. Place an 18mm back-lit cab into the space with the dome facing up.

8. Sew through the beads added in step 6. To close the circle tightly around the dome of the cab, sew through the beads again twice, tying half-hitch knots. Sew through a few more beads to exit an Infinity, and continue through the beadwork to exit the second hole of a mini RounDuo. Sew through the beadwork to exit a mini RounDuo.

NOTE: If you like, stop here and add a loop to make earrings or a lower drop for a necklace.

9. Pick up two 11ºs, a two-hole cabochon, and two 11ºs, and sew through the second hole of the next mini RounDuo. Repeat this stitch five times. Reinforce, exit the two-hole cab, turn, and sew through the open hole of the same two-hole cab.

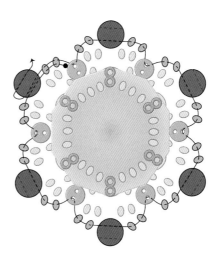

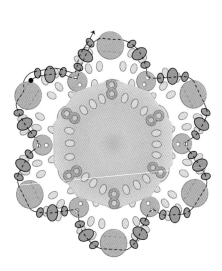

10. Pick up an 11º, an 8º, and an 11º, and sew through first hole of the next mini RounDuo. Pick up an 11º, an 8º, and an 11º, and sew through the open hole of the next two-hole cab. Repeat these stitches five times, and exit the 11º before the two-hole cab.

11. Pick up five 11ºs, and sew through the bead along the outer edge of the beadwork to exit the 11º before the next two-hole cab. Repeat this stitch five times. Reinforce the row, and exit the center 11º above the two-hole cab.

Make four more components.

FINISH THE BRACELET

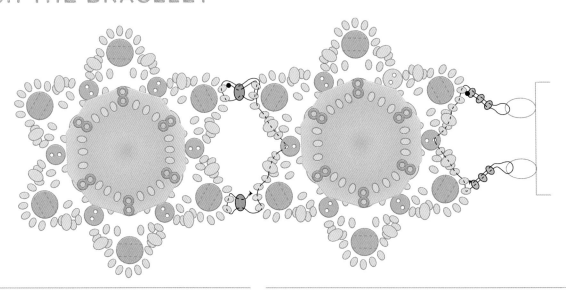

12. Thread a needle on the working thread of a component (exiting a center 11º). Pick up an 8º, and sew through the center 11º and the 11º next to it on a second component. Sew back through the 8º, and continue through the 11º before the center 11º and the center 11º on the first component. Reinforce, sew through the beadwork to the lower section of the second component, and repeat the step. End the threads.

13. Attach a comfortable length of thread to one end of the bracelet, and exit the third 11º after the 8º opposite where the components connect. Pick up three 11ºs and the first loop of the clasp, and sew back through the 11ºs you just added. Continue through the beadwork as shown to exit the corresponding 11º on the other side. Pick up three 11ºs and the second loop of the clasp. Sew back through the 11ºs you just added and into the beadwork. Reinforce the thread path, and end the thread. Repeat on the other end of the bracelet.

FLORET EARRINGS

Sweetly simple, this dainty pair of earrings cleverly showcases the back side of a two-hole cabochon. They're very fast and easy to make.

MAKE THE COMPONENT

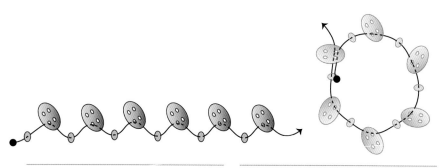

Earrings

 2g 11º seed beads

 12 QuadraLentil beads

12 two-hole cabochons

 2 dagger beads

Pair of earring wires

Beading needle and thread

ORIENTATION

Hole 4

Hole 3 Hole 2

Hole 1

1. Thread a needle on a 50-in. (1.27m) piece of thread, and pick up a repeating pattern of an 11º seed bead and a QuadraLentil bead six times.

2. Sew through all of the beads again to make a circle, leaving a 4-in. (10cm) tail. Sew through all the beads again, tying half-hitch knots. Exit a QuadraLentil. Turn, and sew through the adjacent (second) hole of the same QuadraLentil.

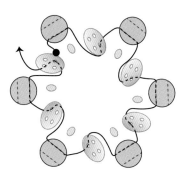

3. Pick up a two-hole cabochon, flat side up and domed side facing away from you, and sew through the corresponding hole of the next QuadraLentil. Repeat this stitch five times. Sew through the entire row, tying half-hitch knots, and exit a QuadraLentil. Turn, and sew through the adjacent (third) hole of the same QuadraLentil.

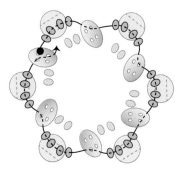

Shared beads

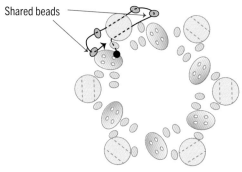

4. Pick up an 11º, and sew though the corresponding hole of the next QuadraLentil. Repeat this stitch five times. Sew through the entire row, and tie a half-hitch knot. Sew through the beads again, and exit a QuadraLentil. Turn, and sew through the the open hole of the same QuadraLentil.

5. Pick up four 11ºs, and sew through the open hole of the next QuadraLentil. Repeat this stitch five times.

Sew through the beads again, tie a half-hitch knot, and exit the second hole of a QuadraLentil.

6. Sew through the 11º and two-hole cab. Pick up two 11ºs, and sew through the open (outer) hole of the two-hole cab. Pick up two 11ºs, and sew through the inner hole of the two-hole cab. (The 11ºs on either side of the inner hole are "shared" beads.)

FINISH THE EARRINGS

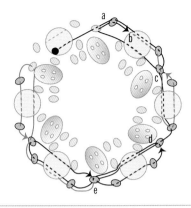

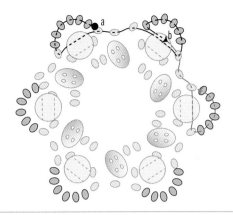

7 **a.** Pick up an 11º, and sew through the outer hole of the next two-hole cab.

b. Pick up two 11ºs, and sew through the inner hole of the same two-hole cab.

c. Sew through the shared bead and the 11º just added, the outer hole of the two-hole cab, and the two 11ºs, exiting from the shared bead. Sew through the inner hole of the next two-hole cab, and pick up two 11ºs. Sew through the outer hole of the same two-hole cab, and pick up an 11º. Sew through the shared bead, the same two-hole cab (inner hole), and the shared bead after. Continue to add beads this way until you are back at the starting point.

8 **a.** Exit the 11º before a two-hole cab's outer hole. Pick up six 11ºs, and sew through an 11º, a two-hole cab (outer hole), and the following 11º.

b. Sew through the shared 11º and the next 11º, two-hole cab, and 11º on the outer hole of the two-hole cab. Pick up six 11ºs, and sew through the 11º, two-hole cab, and 11º group. Repeat this step around the exterior of the entire component. Reinforce, and tie a half-hitch knot. Sew through the beadwork to exit the 11º after a two-hole cab (outer hole).

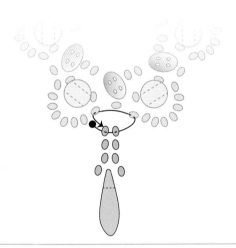

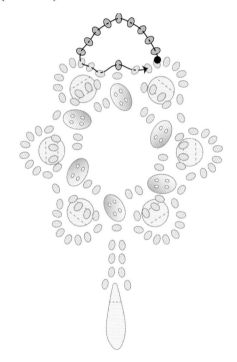

9. Pick up two 11ºs, and sew through the 11º before the next two-hole cab (outer hole). Sew through the 11º you exited, and continue through the first 11º just added. Pick up two 11ºs, and sew through the second 11º just added. Continue around through the 11ºs next to the two-hole cabs, returning back to where you started. Pick up two 11ºs, a dagger bead, and two 11ºs, and sew up into the two beads added as previous rows. Reinforce, and sew through the beadwork to the opposite end of the component. Add the drop: Exit an 11º after the outer hole of the two-hole cab. Pick up two 11ºs, and sew through the 11º, two-hole cab, and adjacent 11º. Pick up two 11ºs, a drop, and two 11ºs, and sew back through the 11ºs, working your way into the beadwork. Reinforce.

10. Exit the 11º after a cab. Pick up an 11º, and sew through the adjacent three 11ºs. Pick up nine 11ºs, and sew through the three 11ºs on the exterior row on the side you started from. Reinforce, end the thread, and attach an earring finding to the loop.

Make a second earring.

LACE DOILY EARRINGS

This light and airy design features circular netting, the same stitch used to create a beaded doily. Two- and three-hole beads in the center allow your beadwork to retain its shape.

Supplies

Earrings

2g 11⁰ seed beads

12 CzechMates two-hole bar beads

12 CzechMates three-hole beam beads

Pair of earring wires

2 4mm jump rings

Beading needle and thread

2 pair of chainnose pliers

MAKE THE EARRINGS

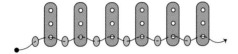

1. Thread a needle on a 50-in. (1.27m) piece of thread, and pick up a repeating pattern of an 11⁰ seed bead and a three-hole beam bead (outer hole) six times.

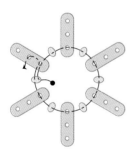

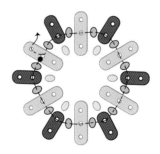

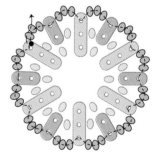

2. Sew through all the beads again to make a circle, leaving a 6-in. (15cm) tail. Retrace the thread path, tying half-hitch knots. Sew through a couple more beads, and exit a beam. Turn, and sew through the center hole of the same beam.

NOTE: You will want the center of this component to be as tight as possible.

3. Pick up an 11⁰, a two-hole bar bead, and an 11⁰, and sew through the center hole of the next beam. Repeat this stitch five times. Reinforce, tie a half-hitch knot, turn, and sew through the open hole of the same beam.

4. Pick up three 11⁰s, and sew through the open hole of the next bar. Pick up three 11⁰s, and sew through the open hole of the next beam. Repeat these stitches five times. Reinforce. Use your fingers to manipulate the three beads in each section to form a picot. Exit the center 11⁰ on one of the picots.

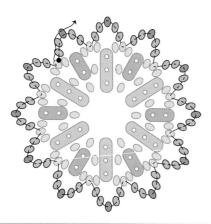

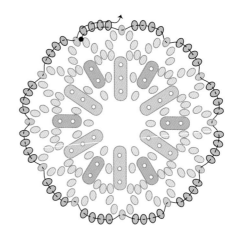

5. Pick up five 11°s (you may add a pattern in this row if you like, using different colored seed beads), and sew through the center 11° in the next set of three. Repeat this stitch 11 times. Exit the center bead (above the bar) of a set of five.

6. Pick up four 11°s, and sew through the center 11° in the next set of five 11°s. Repeat this stitch 11 times. Make sure the beads are placed in proper position. Exit after a set of four 11°s.

NOTE: This round may seem loose, but the next round will fill in the spaces. Do not reinforce steps 5 and 6; you can go back later. The beads should move easily.

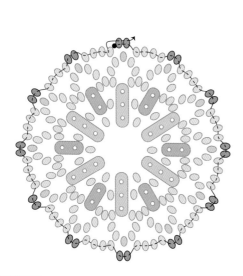

7. Pick up two 11°s, and sew through the next set of four 11°s. Repeat 11 times. Reinforce the outer rows. Exit a set of two 11°s.

8. Add a loop: Pick up nine 11°s, and sew through the set of two 11°s you just exited. Reinforce, and end the threads. Attach an earring wire to the loop with a jump ring. Make a second earring.

LEILANI BRACELET

The name means heavenly flower in Hawaiian. This design evokes visions of sunny beaches in tropical foliage, as GemDuo beads surround a rivoli for maximum sparkle.

MAKE THE COMPONENT

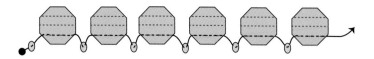

1. Thread a needle on a 60-in. (1.52m) piece of thread, and pick up a repeating pattern of an 11º and an octo bead six times.

NOTE: Check each bead for clear holes as you pick them up. You will not sew through the second and third holes until you have done much more beading. You don't want to find out then the holes are blocked.

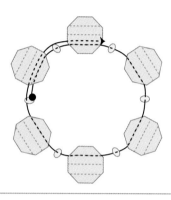

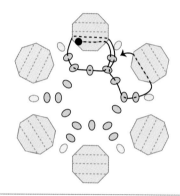

2. Sew through all of the beads again to form a circle, leaving a 5-in. (13cm) tail. Retrace the thread path two more times, tying half-hitch knots, and exit an octo.

3. Make a netted cage around the inside of the bead circle: Pick up five 11ºs, and sew through the same octo. Continue through the first two 11ºs, pick up three 11ºs, and sew through the first hole of the next octo with your needle pointing in the opposite direction. Sew through all five beads, forming a loop around half of the octo, two from the previous octo and three from the current. Change direction and sew through the inner hole of the next octo. Repeat these stitches around the inner holes of octos until all beads have a netted cage. Exit an octo.

4. Turn, and sew through the middle hole of the octo. Pick up an Infinity bead, and sew through the middle hole of the next octo. Repeat these stitches five times. Exit an Infinity.

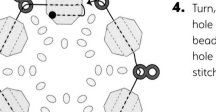

Supplies

Bracelet, 8 in. (20cm)

 8g 11º seed beads

 34 GemDuo beads

 30 6mm Infinity beads

 30 octo three-hole beads

 150 2mm faceted round True 2 beads in **2** colors

5 14mm rivolis

2 4mm jump rings

Clasp

Beading needle and thread

2 pair of chainnose pliers

Pendant
1g 11º seed beads

6 octo beads

12 GemDuo beads

6 Infinity beads

40 2mm faceted round True 2 beads

6 6mm bicone crystals

ORIENTATION

Reverse   Front

Hole 3
Hole 2
Hole 1

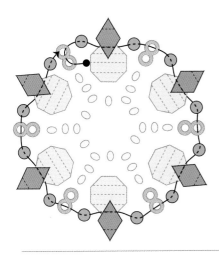

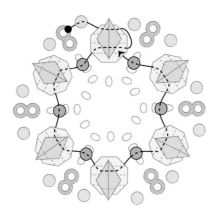

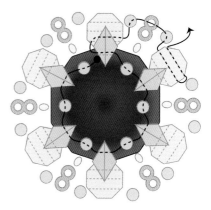

5. Turn, and sew through the second hole of the Infinity. Pick up a color A 2mm faceted round, a GemDuo bead (reverse side), and an A, and sew through the second hole of the next Infinity. Repeat this stitch five times. Continue through the next 2mm and the following GemDuo.

6. Turn, and sew through the open hole of a GemDuo. Pick up an A, and sew through the open hole of the next GemDuo, flipping the GemDuo over as you work, but do not pull the thread tight. Repeat this stitch five times, and exit the second hole of the first GemDuo.

7. Place a rivoli crystal into the space, and sew through the GemDuo and 2mm added in the previous step. Pull the thread closed tightly as you work. Tie a half-hitch knot, and reinforce. Exit the open hole of an octo.

NOTE: You will switch directions in this step two times.

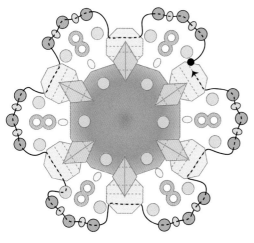

8. Pick up an A, an 11º, a color B 2mm, an 11º, and an A, and sew through the open hole of the next octo. Repeat this stitch five times. Reinforce.

Make four more components.

FINISH THE BRACELET

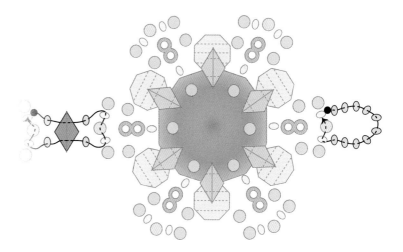

9. Thread a needle on the working thread of a component (exiting an 11º after a 2mm). Pick up an 11º, a GemDuo, and an 11º, and sew through the next 11º, B, and 11º on another component. Pick up an 11º, and sew through the available hole of the GemDuo. Pick up an 11º. Reinforce, and end the thread. Repeat for the remaining components.

10. Make loop for the clasp: Attach a thread on one end of the bracelet, and exit a 11º after a 2mm. Pick up ten 11ºs, and sew through an 11º, a 2mm, and an 11º. Reinforce the thread path, and end the thread. Repeat on the other end of the bracelet. Attach the clasp with jump rings.

MAKE THE PENDANT

1. Follow "Make the component," steps 1–7. Then, pick up a 2mm, an 11º, a 6mm crystal, an 11º, and a 2mm, and sew through the open hole of the next octo. Repeat five times.

2. Sew through the beadwork to exit the 11º after a crystal. Pick up an 11º, a GemDuo (facing up), and five 11ºs, and sew through the second hole of the GemDuo. Pick up an 11º, and sew through the next 11º, crystal, and 11º. Repeat five times.

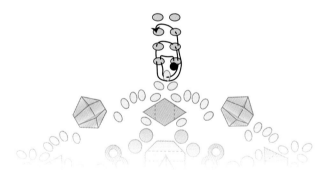

3. Sew through the beadwork to exit the 11º before the second hole of the next GemDuo. Pick up three 11ºs, and sew through the next 11º, crystal, and 11º. Pick up three 11ºs, and sew through the five 11ºs above the GemDuo, exiting the 11º before the second hole of the GemDuo. Repeat this step five times. Reinforce.

4. Make a bail: Exit the 11º at the apex of a GemDuo. Pick up two 11ºs, and sew through the apex bead, then continue through the first 11º just added. Pick up two 11ºs, sew through the 11º and apex bead, and then continue though the first and third 11ºs just added. Pick up two 11ºs, sew through the fourth and second 11ºs added, and then continue through the first, third, and fifth 11ºs added. Continue working in herringbone stitch, adding two beads at a time, for a total of 16 pairs of beads. Then attach the end pair to the same apex bead you started from by passing through it and the final two rows of your herringbone row two or three times to reinforce. End the threads. Add a silk cord to hang the pendant.

STARFISH PENDANT

Seed beads shape the outer layer of this multi-hole beaded pendant into a design similar to a starfish.

MAKE THE PENDANT

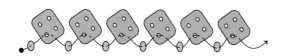

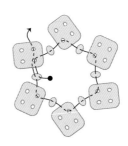

1. Thread a needle on a 60-in. (1.52m) piece of thread, and pick up a repeating pattern of an 11º seed bead and a QuadraTile bead six times.

2. Sew through all the beads again to make a circle, leaving a 4-in. (10cm) tail. Tie a half-hitch knot, sew through all of the beads again, and exit a QuadraTile. Turn, and sew through the adjacent (second) hole of the same QuadraTile.

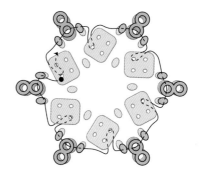

3. Pick up an 11º, a mini Infinity bead, and an 11º, and sew through the corresponding hole of the next QuadraTile. Repeat this stitch five times. Exit a QuadraTile, turn, and sew through the adjacent (third) hole of the same QuadraTile.

4. Flip the beadwork over. Pick up an 11º, an Infinity (shown in green for clarity), and an 11º, and sew through the corresponding third hole of the next QuadraTile. Repeat this stich five times. Reinforce, tie a half-hitch knot, and exit a QuadraTile. Turn, and sew through the open (fourth) hole of the QuadraTile.

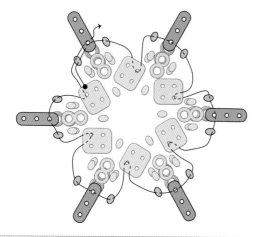

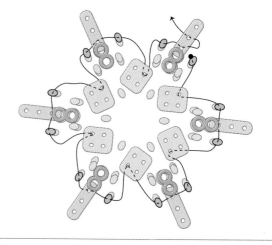

5. Pick up an 11º, a beam bead (outer hole), and an 11º, and sew through the last open (fourth) hole of the next QuadraTile. Repeat this stitch five times, and exit a beam.

6. Flip the beadwork over. Pick up an 11º, and sew through the nearest hole of the QuadraTile. Pick up an 11º, and sew through the same hole of the beam. Repeat these stitches five times. Exit the beam, turn, and sew through the middle hole of the beam.

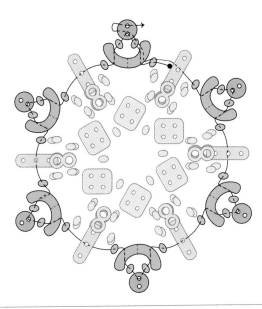

7. Pick up an 11º, an Arcos par Puca bead (outer hole, curved side), an 11º, a mini Es-o bead, an 11º, the second hole of the same Arcos, and an 11º, and sew through the middle hole of the next beam. Repeat this stitch five times. Exit the Es-o, turn, and sew through the second hole of the same Es-o.

NOTE: At this point, carefully move beads along the thread into the correct position.

8. Work on the side of the pendant that is comfortable. Pick up four 11ºs and an 8º seed bead, and sew through the open hole of the Infinity. Pick up an 8º and four 11ºs, and sew through the open hole of the next Es-o. Repeat these stitches five times. Exit the 11º after the Es-o.

9. Flip the beadwork over. Pick up three 11ºs and an 8º, and sew through the open hole of the Infinity. Pick up an 8º and three 11ºs, and sew through the open hole of the Es-o and the 11º after it. Repeat these stitches five times. Exit the 11º after the Es-o.

10. Pick up three 11ºs and an 8º, and sew through the open hole of the next beam. Pick up an 8º and three 11ºs, and sew through the next 11º, Es-o, and 11º three-bead set. Repeat these stitches five times. Exit the 11º before the Es-o.

11. Pick up three 11ºs, and sew through the next four 11ºs, 8ºs, outer hole of the beam, 8º, and four 11ºs, and repeat five times. Reinforce this row. Exit the center 11º above an Es-o.

12. Add a loop: Pick up nine 11ºs, and sew through the 11º the thread is exiting. Reinforce, and end the thread.

Supplies

Pendant

4g 11º seed beads

2g 8º seed beads

6 QuadraTile beads

6 CzechMates three-hole bead beads

12 mini Infinity beads

6 4mm mini Es-o beads

6 Arcos par Puca beads

Clasp

Beading needle and thread

ORIENTATION

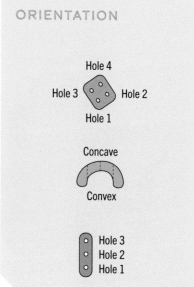

Hole 4

Hole 3   Hole 2

Hole 1

Concave

Convex

Hole 3
Hole 2
Hole 1

EDWARDIAN BRACELET

Make a dazzling design with multi-hole beads. An alternate pair of earrings can be created from half of the finished bracelet component.

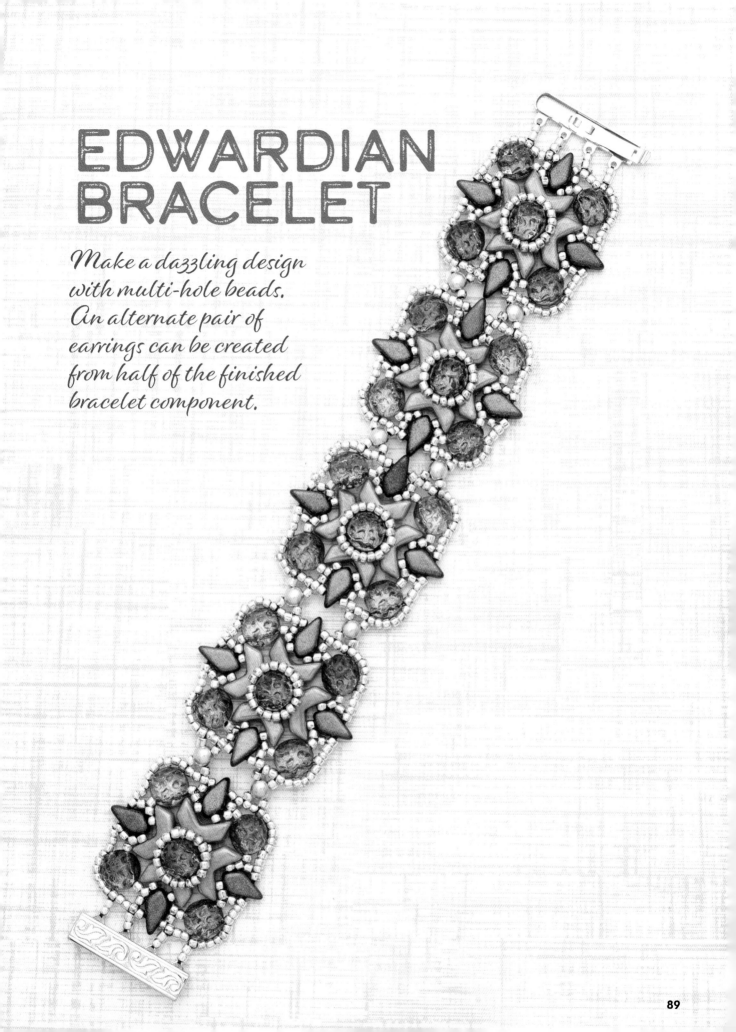

MAKE THE COMPONENT

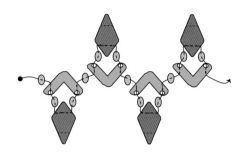

Supplies

Bracelet, 8 in. (20cm)

○ **6g** 11º seed beads

○ **3g** 8º seed beads,

◆ **20** Kite beads

⌄ **20** Chevron beads

⬭ **25** 7mm two-hole baroque cabochons

◉ **12** 4mm RounDuo beads

4-loop clasp

Beading needle and thread

1. Thread a needle on a 60-in. (1.52m) piece of thread, and pick up an 11º seed bead, a Chevron bead (outer hole), an 11º, a Kite bead (wide end), and an 11º. Sew through the second hole of the Chevron. Repeat these stitches three times.

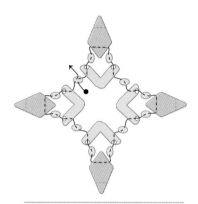

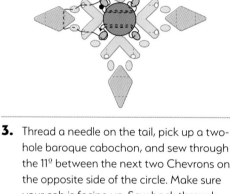

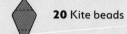

ORIENTATION

Wide end   Tip end

Tip end   Wide end

2. Sew through all the beads again to make a tight circle, leaving a 14-in. (36cm) tail. Tie a half-hitch knot between Chevrons.

3. Thread a needle on the tail, pick up a two-hole baroque cabochon, and sew through the 11º between the next two Chevrons on the opposite side of the circle. Make sure your cab is facing up. Sew back through the same hole of the cab and the 11º you first exited. Sew through the beads to exit the next 11º adjacent to the second hole of cab. Sew through the cab and the nearest 11º. Turn, and sew back through the cab.

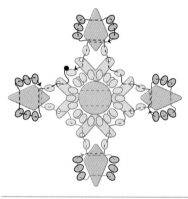

4. Pick up three 11ºs, and sew through the first hole of the cab. Pick up three 11ºs, and sew through the second hole of the cab plus the three 11ºs.

5. Pick up six 11ºs, and sew through the next set of three. Pick up six 11ºs, and sew through the first set of three. Reinforce well. Tie a knot, and end the thread.

6. Thread a needle on the working thread, and sew through the beadwork to exit the wide end of a Kite, pick up three 11ºs, and sew through the tip end of the same Kite. Pick up three 11ºs, and sew through the wide end of the same Kite. Sew through the beadwork to exit the next Kite (wide end). Repeat these stitches three times. Reinforce.

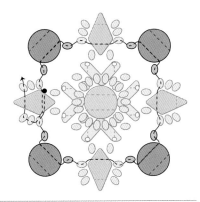

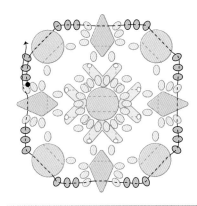

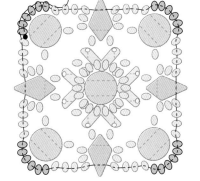

7. Exit the first 11º after the wide end of the Kite. Pick up an 11º, a two-hole cab, and an 11º, and sew through the next 11º, Kite (wide end), and 11º. Repeat this stitch three times. Reinforce, and exit a Kite and three 11ºs, the tip of the Kite, and the folllowing 11º.

8. Pick up three 11ºs, and sew through the open hole of the next two-hole cab. Pick up three 11ºs, and sew through the 11º, Kite (tip end), and 11º. Repeat these stitches three times. Exit the last 11º before the two-hole cab.

9. Pick up five 11ºs, and sew through the beads along the outer edge to exit the last 11º before the next cab. Repeat this stitch three times. Reinforce, and exit the third 11º before the Kite's tip end.

Make four more tiles to finish the bracelet.

FINISH THE BRACELET

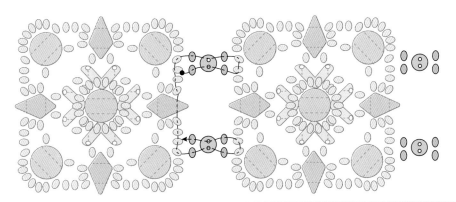

10. Thread a needle on the working thread of a component (exiting the third 11º before the Kite's tip end). Pick up an 11º, a mini RounDuo bead, and an 11º, and sew through the fourth and third beads before the Kite tip on another component. Pick up an 11º, sew through the open hole of the mini RounDuo, pick up an 11º, and sew through the fourth and third beads on the first component. Attach a clasp by exiting the fifth 11º before the Kite's tip end. Pick up two 11ºs and the first loop of the clasp, then sew back through the 11ºs just added, and continue into the opposite side of the fifth 11ºs. Reinforce, and sew through the beadwork to the second 11º before the Kite's tip end. Pick up two 11ºs and the second loop of the clasp, and sew back through the 11ºs just added and the second 11º from the Kite's tip. Reinforce. Sew through the beadwork to the second 11º after the Kite's tip end. Pick up two 11ºs and the third loop of the clasp, and then sew back through the 11º. Reinforce. Sew through the bead-work to the fifth 11º after the Kite's tip. Pick up two 11ºs and the last loop of the clasp, then sew back through the 11º and the fifth 11º after the Kite's tip. Reinforce the thread path, and end the thread. Repeat on the other end of the bracelet to attach the other half of the clasp.

MANDALA PENDANT

Sewing 'round and 'round in a circle is almost like meditation—especially in this simple, yet stunning, pendant.

MAKE THE PENDANT

1. Thread a needle on a 60-in. (1.52m) piece of thread, and pick up a repeating pattern of an 11º seed bead and an Infinity bead eight times.

2. Sew through all of the beads three more times, tying half-hitch knots as needed. Exit an Infinity. Turn, and sew through the open hole of the same Infinity.

Supplies

Pendant

〇 **3g** 11º seed beads

〇 **2g** 8º seed beads,

⊙ **8** QuadraLentil beads

8 **20** 4x8mm Infinity beads

⬤ ⬤ **16** 6mm two-hole cabochons

2 4mm jump rings

Beading needle and thread

ORIENTATION

Hole 4 ⊙ Hole 3
Hole 2 ⊙ Hole 1

3. Pick up an 11º, a QuadraLentil bead, and an 11º, and sew through the open hole of the next Infinity. Repeat this stitch seven times. Exit a QuadraLentil, turn, and sew through the adjacent (second) hole of the same QuadraLentil.

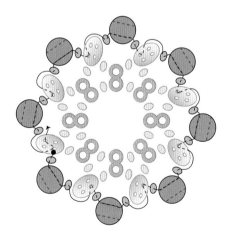

4. Pick up an 11º, a two-hole cabochon, and an 11º, and sew through the corresponding second hole of the next QuadraLentil. Repeat this stitch seven times. Reinforce, and tie a knot. Exit the QuadraLentil, turn, and sew through the adjacent (third) hole of the same QuadraLentil.

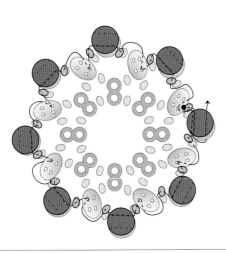

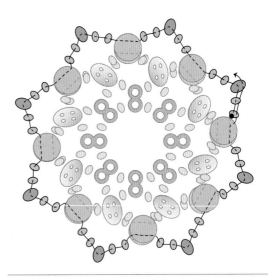

5. Flip the beadwork over. Pick up an 11º, a two-hole cab, and an 11º, and sew through the corresponding hole of the next QuadraLentil. Repeat this stitch seven times. Reinforce the row. Exit the two-hole cab, turn, and sew through the other hole of the same bead.

6. Pick up two 11ºs, an 8º, and two 11ºs, and sew through the corresponding hole of the next two-hole cab. Repeat this stitch seven times. Exit an 8º.

7. Flip the beadwork over. Pick up two 11ºs, and sew through the open hole of the next two-hole cab on this side of the beadwork. Pick up two 11ºs, and sew through the next 8º. Repeat these stitches seven times. Reinforce, and exit an 8º.

8. Pick up 13 11ºs, and sew through the same 8º the thread is exiting (opposite side). Reinforce, and end the thread.

ACKNOWLEDGMENTS

Thanks to my family, Terry, Dakota, and Autumn Coulton, for putting up with me. Thanks to the Bead Society of Eastern Pennsylvania, including Bernadette, Cindy, Valarie, Jeanette, and Bev, for proofreading and testing my projects. Thank you to BeadSmith and the Inspiration Squad, including Leslie Pope and Leslie Rogalski, and also Potomac beads for supplying samples of new beads for me to use.

ABOUT THE AUTHOR

Patricia Parker is an award-winning seed bead artist. Her work has been published in advertisements, books, and magazines. A former bead store owner, Patti's passion for beading has spanned three decades. She studied Fine Art at Kutztown University and holds certification from the GIA as an Accredited Jewelry Professional. A participant in the Battle of the BeadSmith for four years, she has recently joined the BeadSmith Inspiration Squad.

CREATE GORGEOUS STITCHED JEWELRY!

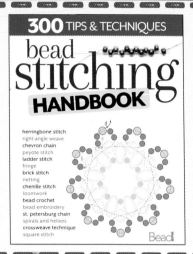

Bead Stitching Handbook
Discover information, instructions, and hundreds of tips for the 15 major bead stitches.
#67910 • $19.99

Two-Hole Bead Stitching
Experienced stitchers and adventurous beginners alike will enjoy projects featuring tiles, bricks, SuperDuos, pyramid beads and more!
#67913 • $22.99

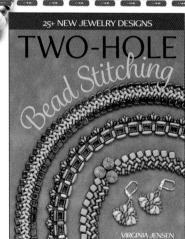

Beader's Guide: Peyote Stitch
Explore all the possibilities of the beader's most popular stitch in 20+ classic and contemporary styles.
#67916 • $19.99

Buy now from your favorite craft or bead shop!
Shop at JewelryandBeadingStore.com

Sales tax where applicable.

P35633